Additional Praise for *The Age of Dignity*

"Joining a storyteller's ear to an organizer's spirit, Ai-jen Poo offers a practical guide to creating a more caring America that is more prosperous and just—for immigrant women hired to care no less than elder boomers in need."

—Eileen Boris, co-author of *Caring for America*
and Hull Professor of Feminist Studies
at the University of California, Santa Barbara

"Ai-jen understands as well as anyone that the nature of work is changing. She is one of the smartest and most empathetic advocates in America, and *The Age of Dignity* has the solutions we need to ensure workers of any age have the independence and dignity they deserve."

—Sara Horowitz, founder and executive director
of the Freelancers Union

"Ai-jen Poo is among our most compelling social movement leaders. In *The Age of Dignity,* a most thoughtful and readable book, she invites us to join arms and reshape our economy and our culture."

—Ambassador Swanee Hunt, chair of Hunt Alternatives
and Eleanor Roosevelt Lecturer in Public Policy at
Harvard University's Kennedy School of Government

"Within the next twenty-five years, tens of millions of baby boomers are going to become frail and need long-term services and supports. How will we live? Who will care for us? In *The Age of Dignity,* Ai-jen Poo presents a bold and inspiring vision for the future—one that can unite caregivers, older adults and their families, advocates, and policy makers to join forces to address the extraordinary care challenge that is clearly coming."

—Jim Firman, president and CEO
of the National Council on Aging

THE AGE OF DIGNITY

Preparing for the Elder Boom
in a Changing America

AI-JEN POO
WITH ARIANE CONRAD

THE NEW PRESS

NEW YORK
LONDON

Requests for permission to reproduce selections from this book should be mailed to:
Permissions Department, The New Press,
120 Wall Street, 31st floor, New York, NY 10005.

Published in the United States by The New Press, New York, 2015
Distributed by Perseus Distribution

LIBRARY OF CONGRESS CATALOGING-IN-PUBLICATION DATA
Poo, Ai-jen.
The age of dignity : preparing for the elder boom in a changing America /
Ai-jen Poo, with Ariane Conrad.
pages   cm
Includes bibliographical references and index.
ISBN 978-1-62097-038-6 (hardcover : alk. paper) — ISBN 978-1-62097-046-1
(e-book)   1. Older people—Care—United States.   2. Older people—
Nursing home care—United States.   3. Older people—Services for—United
States.   4. Population aging—United States.   I. Title.
HV1461.P66 2015
361.60973—dc23   2014029148

The New Press publishes books that promote and enrich public discussion and
understanding of the issues vital to our democracy and to a more equitable world.
These books are made possible by the enthusiasm of our readers; the support of
a committed group of donors, large and small; the collaboration of our many
partners in the independent media and the not-for-profit sector; booksellers, who
often hand-sell New Press books; librarians; and above all by our authors.

www.thenewpress.com

Composition by dix!
This book was set in Fournier MT

Printed in the United States of America

2 4 6 8 10 9 7 5 3 1

For the millions of women whose life's work is caring for others. Thank you for doing the work that makes all other work possible.

For my maternal grandmother and paternal grandfather. Your experiences and all that I've learned from you light the way forward.

CONTENTS

THE AGE OF DIGNITY

INTRODUCTION

Caring Across Generations

My father's father, Liang Shao Pu, lived to the age of ninety-three. A lifelong student and then teacher of tai chi and a diehard *Wheel of Fortune* fan, he had a slow, deep-throated laugh that never failed to infect my sister and me, sending us into spasms of giggles. After moving from Taiwan to the United States to be close to his children and grandchildren, my grandfather often picked us up from school, the silhouette of his baseball cap visible from down the block. He was never late.

My grandfather quietly sustained the heartbreaks of my parents' divorce, the passing of most of his friends, and then the loss of his wife of more than forty years. After my grandmother's stroke, she could no longer care for herself. With tremendous courage and love, for years he cooked every meal, talked to her, and kept her comfortable until the end. One of my greatest regrets in life is that we did not provide him with the same comfort and care in the final moments of his life.

After repeated strokes, my grandfather's condition had deteriorated to the point that my dad no longer felt capable of providing the support he needed to stay at home and could not find appropriate home care support, so my grandfather was placed in a nursing home, against his wishes. I visited my grandfather there before he passed away.

My grandfather's bed was along a wall in a large, dark room with six other people, half of whom were completely silent, while the other half expressed their misery in loud, painful cries. The room lights were kept off, while a sickly fluorescent light in the hallway flickered. The place smelled like mold and death. It was my heart-wrenching introduction to dehumanizing institutional care.

When I arrived at his bedside, my grandfather was distressed. He believed the nursing home staff was trying to poison him. He had not slept or eaten for some time. He was frightened and in pain. He was a shadow of the person I knew growing up. I was furious and devastated.

After three months, he passed away in that facility. I almost feel as though he died the moment he arrived there; his dignity was stripped away upon entry. My father, my sister, and I will always regret that my grandfather's final hours and ultimately his death were so lacking in comfort and beauty. He meant so much to us. I so wish we had been able to keep him at home.

I'm far from alone in my aversion to nursing homes. Nearly 90 percent of Americans feel institutions are not the appropriate place for elders to spend their final moments, months, or years. The great majority of us want to live and age at home. The question is how, exactly, we can manage that.

America is about to experience an "elder boom," a direct result of the baby boom of 1946 to 1964. We have more senior citizens in America today than we've had at any time in our history. Every eight seconds an American turns sixty-five; that's more than ten thousand people per day, almost 4 million per year. A century ago, just about 3 percent of the population was sixty-five or older. Today more than 13 percent of Americans are over sixty-five, and by 2030, the number will be 20 percent. The 5 million Americans older than eighty-five, our country's fastest-growing demographic, will number 11.5 million by 2035. Because of advances in health care and technology, people are living longer than ever, often into their nineties or breaking one hundred.

Let's remember: *people getting older is not a crisis; it's a blessing.* We're living longer; the question is how we should live. As a country, we have to figure out how to embrace this demographic shift with grace. Just as the baby boom brought with it incredible power and opportunity, so does the coming elder boom.

One thing we know is that the longer people live, the more likely they are to need assistance. Seventy percent of people aged sixty-five or older need some form of support. By 2050, the total number of individuals needing long-term care and personal assistance is projected to grow from 12 million to 27 million. It is often assumed that women will absorb these tasks, as they have for much of our country's history, but that is not going to happen in twenty-first-century America. Most households today are dual income, which means there is no one at home full-time; at the same time, more and more American households have both children and aging parents who need support and care every day. The need for professional caregivers is skyrocketing.

Aging at home necessitates home care workers. Yet the

3 million people currently in the home care workforce cannot meet even the current need, let alone the demand for care that will accompany the elder boom. We will need at least 1.8 million additional home care workers in the next decade. As a result, caregiving, specifically home care, is the fastest growing of all occupations in the nation.[1] By 2018, demand for home care workers will increase by more than 90 percent.[2] Many of the existing eldercare workers are low-income African American and immigrant women who are faced with innumerable challenges, among them low wages, long hours, and inadequate training. Of the one-quarter of today's home care workers who were born outside the United States, about half are undocumented, which means that fear of deportation puts these workers under further stress. These conditions have led to high turnover in the industry, which hurts everyone: elders, their families, and the workers themselves.

Many of these issues also have profound implications for people of all ages with disabilities. With the birth of the disability rights movement in the 1960s and 1970s, independent living replaced institutionalization as the clear preference of people with disabilities. Alongside assistive technologies, it is home care workers, predominantly known in the community of people with disabilities as "personal attendants," who enable many people with disabilities to manage their personal care, maintain a home, have a job, go to school, and participate in other aspects of independent living. According to the U.S. Census, in 2000, an estimated 13 million Americans with disabilities were living independently in their communities. The concerns and stories of people with disabilities are and should be the subject of many books, and while these topics are deeply connected, this book's focus is the aging of America—the challenge and opportunity of this demographic moment.

Many Americans currently struggle to afford the care they need. On average, a home health aide hired through an agency costs approximately $21 per hour, the cost of an assisted living facility averages $3,300 per month, and a semiprivate room in a nursing home costs $6,200 per month. Yet the average Social Security check amounts to just $1,230 per month, and Medicare provides little if any support for home-based care. How can elders or people with disabilities remain at home and live independently without sufficient support or funding? Our country has not adequately accounted for the caregiving we need. Yet home care is the future.

By 2010, we at the National Domestic Workers Alliance, an organization I helped found in 2007 to support the nearly invisible workforce employed inside homes across America, began hearing more and more workers asking for training in eldercare. Although these workers had been hired as nannies and housekeepers, they were now being called upon to provide home care for their employers' aging parents, too.

In response, in 2011, together with our sister organization Jobs with Justice, we launched Caring Across Generations, an initiative that addresses two of the major social issues of our time: widespread unemployment and the coming need for care for the nation's expanding aging population. At the same time that millions of people in the United States are struggling to survive long-term unemployment, there are far too few workers who are positioned and prepared to provide care for the growing number of elders and people with disabilities. The demographic shift creates a moment when we can set in place a system to affirm the dignity of people at every stage of life and in every walk of life, and create millions of good jobs in the process.

Caring Across Generations, led jointly by twenty organizations representing caregivers, care consumers, and their families, is a national movement to embrace our changing demographics, particularly the aging of America, and an opportunity to strengthen our intergenerational and caregiving relationships. We're calling for an innovative approach to care, rooted in our homes and communities, that brings us all together and offers support to everyone involved.

As for Me

People always ask how I arrived at the work I do with domestic workers. When they do, I immediately think of my mom. While she was not a domestic worker, I can't conjure a single image of my mother resting during my whole childhood. She learned English, she worked and went to school, and she was the only one in her class at medical school with two children. I can remember her dropping me off at day care, picking me up, making dinner, cleaning the house, ironing clothes. But I can't remember her ever relaxing. I don't think she saw that as an option. It was assumed that even though she had a PhD in chemistry as well as an MD, and went on to become an oncologist at two of the top cancer centers in the nation, she would still be primarily responsible for feeding, clothing, and getting me and my sister to day care and school. Even today, at the age of sixty-four, perhaps out of habit, she doesn't stop. She is always up the earliest, and while she goes to bed earlier these days, for the entire day she is going, going, going.

As a young person, I saw women as key to everything working well, yet our systems were not working for women. So I joined my first women's organization in high school and have not looked back since. No question: my dedication to women was inspired by my mother and my mother's mother—the brilliant, strong, beautiful women who cared for me. They were innovators and trailblazers, yet so much of their work seemed to go unnoticed and unappreciated. They sacrificed so much, even their own health at times, to work and to care for us, the way so many women and family caregivers do. Today I witness the domestic workers in my organization caring for the families they work for and, after a long day, returning home to care for their own families, surviving with less support and fewer resources than my mother had. Working women of all walks of life face impossible choices. I hear and collect their stories everywhere I go; you will find many in the pages of this book. They help expand my sense of what's possible, and they have helped me through my own difficult choices.

"Well, you should have stopped traveling." That's the first thing a friend of mine said to me after my miscarriage. Like millions of other women in America and around the world, I've been through the quiet, enigmatic labyrinth of fertility treatments and all the heartache associated with the process. I know the impossible choices women face while deciding which work trips to cancel in preparation for fertility treatments, the desperate searches for medical laboratories while traveling, the sleepless nights filled with guilt, self-doubt, and shame that come along with making a choice—whatever it is.

And I know what it means to need to focus on one area of care and not have a whole lot left for anything or anyone else. At every stage of my struggle with fertility, my mom always told me, "We'll be okay." What if she wasn't okay? What if she needed me? What if I had to travel for her? I never stop feeling the need to prepare for that moment and what it would mean for my ability to care across generations, in both directions.

Almost all our major laws and systems for care are based on standards and demographics from another era. However, today, from what I see all over the country and in many places across the globe, we're finally moving from impossible, false choices to real choices. People are already adapting. In their experiences and stories, many of which I've tried to include in this book, we can see the future we need to create. We can see the way we need to adapt the system.

With some course corrections in our culture and in our institutions, we can have the care infrastructure that will enable us to live our full potential. We've adapted many systems before, changing our country for the next era, and while it's never going to be easy to be the mom, partner, or daughter that you want to be, at least the very material and practical elements of that complexity can be relieved by a solid, reliable care infrastructure.

This is a book of problems finding solutions. When they do, it will give us all real choices—no matter who we are or what role we play at any given time—choices that enable us to be free, to love, to have peace of mind. The moral of this story is that a caring America is entirely within reach.

Care is something we do; it's something we want; it's something we can improve. But more than anything, it's the solution to the personal and economic challenges we face in this country. It doesn't just heal or comfort people individually; it really is going to save us all.

PART I

A Changing America Needs Care

The questions of eldercare in America loom large: how many of us will need it? Who will do it? Who will pay for it? What type of care do we mean: someone to clean and cook, to lift spirits or provide emotional support, to help dress or lift an aging body? What qualifies someone to provide care, and where is care best given: at home or in specialized institutions? For how long will care be needed? Can we afford dignified care? What is the cost, moral and economic, of not supporting it?

It is time that we really see and listen to elders, especially those over the age of eighty-five, the fastest-growing sector of America's population; the family members who care for them, particularly who care for both their children and their elder parents; and the workforce of professional caregivers on whom we rely. The more we consider the meaning and importance of care, the more we realize that all of us, all 314 million Americans, all 7 billion residents of planet Earth, are caught up in this issue.

I think of a walk I took the other day with my writing partner, Ariane. During the months we worked together on this book we took many walks, leaving our laptops behind to talk through ideas as we breathed in fresh air. This particular day was in late winter; the palette of the world was mostly the gray of the cloudy sky, the brown of the ground and the curled leaves, and the black of the tree trunks and the surface of the lake. Ariane's small rescued dog, Maizie, bounded ahead, taking her usual delight even in the bleak surroundings, and when we caught up with her sniffing something in the leaves, I pointed down.

"Look, Maizie found the first crocus!"

It was delicate, not quite open, and the palest purple.

We smiled and resumed our walking and talking, and then Ariane grabbed my arm.

"Look, Ai-jen, they're everywhere!"

As if by magic, suddenly we could see the pale purple flowers poking up through the ground everywhere we looked. All it took was opening our eyes to the first one for us to notice that they were everywhere, all around us.

This is what the issue of care is like. Once our eyes have been opened, we see it everywhere.

1

THE ELDER BOOM

Even after all this time,
the sun never says to the earth
"you owe me."
Look what happens
with a love like that.
It lights up the whole sky.

—Hafiz

"I'm not afraid of dying," my grandma tells me. "But I am afraid of getting dementia or having a stroke. That's really scary—the idea of not being able to find my way home, or not remembering my own children. But when you get older you never know what will happen."

My mother's mother. She has always been my greatest teacher.

"Every time you laugh, you extend your life an extra day, so you may as well laugh a lot" is one of her standard pieces of wisdom. I learned that from her, and now she's teaching me about what it looks like to age with humor, grace, and dignity. Her experience of old age so far, surrounded by care and support, stands as a beautiful contrast to the heartbreaking example of my paternal grandfather, whose story I shared in the introduction.

Xue Mei Sun is an immigrant from China, living in Los Angeles County with her two adult sons and husband. She works as a caregiver for my grandmother and is an invaluable presence in my family. We are a team, and my grandmother is at the heart of it all, living life fully on her terms at eighty-seven.

PHOTOGRAPH BY MICHELE ASSELIN

I was her first grandchild. From ages one to two I lived under her care in Taiwan, because my mom, at age twenty-five, was still finishing her graduate studies at Carnegie Mellon and working to put herself through school. Even after I came back to the United States to attend preschool, I spent many childhood summers back in Taiwan in my grandmother's care, accompanying her to the market in the morning and watching her prepare food while tracking the flight patterns of outrageously large cockroaches. Munching on the American Pringles I carefully rationed to last my stay, I listened to her stories about all of our relatives. Like the sun in the center of my family's universe, she was, and still is, the one around whom we all revolve.

My grandmother was born in 1926 and raised in Anhui Province in China. She lived through World War II and the civil war that caused her to flee China for Taiwan, where she lived and worked for more than fifty years, raising three children: my mom (the eldest) and two sons.

"I never take anything for granted. I lived through the war [World War II], so I know what it means to suffer. When I was a child, I was really unhealthy. I had malaria, typhoid, many dangerous illnesses, and I never died. I can withstand a lot. Back then, we had no choice. I look at the positive of everything. Whatever the situation is, I always try to look on the bright side."

She worked as a nurse in a clinic from 1948 until 1983, when she became the clinic administrator. Thanks in large part to her hard work and sacrifice, all three of her children completed college and received financial aid to attend graduate programs in the United States. They all settled in the United States, had children, and put down roots in their new home.

At first, my grandmother stayed in Taiwan after her retirement, until the pull of more time with her grandchildren became irresistible. In 2000 she and my grandfather sold their small apartment in Taipei and moved to the United States. After living with my mom and then my uncles, they decided to settle in Los Angeles, in a Chinese retirement community on Valley Boulevard in Alhambra, where groceries and prepared food are all within walking distance and most people speak Chinese. Soon after moving there, my grandfather had a stroke that left the right side of his body paralyzed.

My grandmother, while still extremely vibrant and healthy, had broken her hip not long before the stroke, so she was not able to lift anything heavy. My grandfather needed help with everything: getting out of bed, getting dressed, bathing, eating; every daily activity of life required the assistance of a physically strong person. So they asked around, and my grandmother found an ad for a home care agency in the Chinese newspaper. She contacted the agency and hired a home care provider. My grandparents had two care providers come through, and for various reasons, each stayed for only a year or so. Mrs. Sun was their third, and she became, as they say, like part of the family.

With Mrs. Sun's assistance, for the following two years after the stroke, my grandfather was able to live with my grandmother at home, as he had for more than fifty years of marriage. He was able to eat the food my grandmother cooked, in the style of Anhui Province, where they're both from, and though he couldn't talk much because the paralysis from the stroke impacted his speech, he could still sit at the table and be a part of our dinner conversations. He still had questions for us that Mrs. Sun or my grandmother could interpret for us. Thanks to the care team of Mrs. Sun and my grandmother, my grandfather was able to live in the comfort of his own very clean home until his second stroke landed him in the hospital for two months.

After my grandfather was hospitalized, I flew out from New York to visit him in California. A range of emotions cycled through me as I made my way to the hospital: guilt, regret, fear, longing, and appreciation. I was sorry that I hadn't been to the hospital sooner, that I hadn't visited enough over the past four years since his first stroke. My flight across the country was a long, slow stream of memories of my grandfather from my childhood, when I spent my summers living with him and my grandmother in Taiwan. I had a vivid memory of him sweeping the apartment floors in his underwear in the hot summer evenings with a handmade straw broom, asking me whether I had washed my hands. Cleanliness and order were always very important to him, and he insisted that everyone in the family wash their hands repeatedly throughout the day.

When I finally arrived at the door of the hospital room, the first person I saw was Mrs. Sun. The hospital was more than an hour's drive from Mrs. Sun's home, yet she came every day, usually twice a day, to see my grandfather. She arrived in the morning and stayed for the greater part of the day to help him with his needs as she always had—with eating and bathing—and to keep him company. Then she would go home for dinner with her own family. Most nights, she would return to the hospital after dinner just to check on him and my grandmother.

There in the hospital Mrs. Sun was combing my grandfather's hair at his bedside, with the same black plastic comb that he had used for years. My grandfather had a beautiful head of hair; he was one of those blessed men who didn't lose his hair as he grew older and whose hair didn't gray until much later in life. He took great pride in his hair, and I remember watching him comb it perfectly into place when I was a child. Mrs. Sun knew that combing his hair was just the thing to help him find calm in the midst of the most frightening transition that a person can make, into the unknown.

My grandfather wasn't awake when I arrived. I washed my hands before sitting down at his bedside to start my good-byes. I wish I had been able to stay so I could have been there when he passed away several weeks later, but I took comfort in knowing that my grandmother and Mrs. Sun were with him at the very end.

Five years later, Mrs. Sun still comes to my grandmother's home every week to help her with cleaning and chores, so that she can live independently, in the same apartment she shared with my grandfather.

Today, at eighty-seven, my grandmother looks more like she's in her late sixties or early seventies. Her black hair is well coiffed thanks to regular Saturday visits to the salon. She is still walking upright and leads an active life. She has her favorite Chinese soap operas. She plays mah-jong with her friends—she's a mah-jong shark—and goes to church twice a week. "I'm glad to be living on my own, able to take care of myself for the most part. I know I need support for some things. My training as a nurse allows me to understand what's happening with my body and how to take care of my health perhaps more than other people. I have friends who are constantly at the doctor, and constantly in need of someone at their side. Most people my age are not as independent. I do need Mrs. Sun. If I need to go to the doctor, or get my hair done, she comes with me. Going to church, she or her son takes me."

Having spent four years of her life worrying about my grandfather, and the rest of her life supporting her children and grandchildren, now that she's in her eighties, my grandma is living life on her terms. Mrs. Sun helps make that possible.

"I do worry about her," my mom says about my grandma, "but I worry about her less since Grandpa passed away. When Grandpa was still around, after he had his stroke, your grandma sacrificed a lot. He couldn't do anything for himself. She essentially took over attending to everything he needed at night after his caregiver left. That took a huge toll on her. She had to get up throughout the night. For four years, she could barely get sleep. Now that he's passed, she's on her own and has more flexibility to be active and take care of her own health."

My mother is sixty-three and counting the days to her own retirement. She longs to move to Alhambra and spend every day with my grandmother, who is also her best friend. When they're together, my mother comes alive. She laughs more—because my grandmother demands it. It's like my mom gets an extra battery when my grandmother's around. When they're not together, they talk on the phone just about every day, chatting about the weather, updates from my sister and me, and stories about different people with illnesses. Between my mom's work as an oncologist and my grandmother's life in the retirement community, they have a lot of stories about sickness, caregiving, and dying.

"I hope that I have saved enough money so that I can find someone as good as Mrs. Sun when I become incapacitated," my mom tells me. "She is a true caregiver."

"What do you mean by that, Mom?" I ask her.

"You can feel it. It's subtle, but you can feel it in every aspect of the interaction. If you have the right heart, and the passion for taking care of people, that's the most important thing you need. Caring is the most important part of care. Sounds funny, but all the other skills can be learned. But it's hard to train someone to care."

As a doctor, my mother is a passionate caregiver for her patients, and as a result, her patients' battles with cancer have been a constant part of our lives. Every Christmas, my mother receives a flood of Christmas cards from her patients and their families, all with updates about how life moves forward, sprinkled with memories of some very difficult times and heartbreaking losses. One family, the Golats, have become like extended family to my mom. Their late daughter, Kelly, died at twenty-five after a valiant battle with a brutal form of melanoma. Every year for more than ten years, the first weekend in October, the family organizes Run for Kelly, a 5K run that begins and ends at Kelly's high school in the Poconos and helps raise funds for melanoma research. My mom attends every year and brings a team of volunteer doctors to do skin cancer screenings for the runners who participate.

I attend most years to keep her company and even attempt to run the 5K. Kelly was a runner herself, and among the patients to whom my mother became the most attached. At the end of the run, there is a cookout for participants and a short program when winners in each age-group are announced. My mother always says a few words about Kelly and then shares updates on her work to find a cure. It's always emotional, one of those moments when I'm filled with pride as I'm reminded of the tremendous relationships of care and connection that my mother has with her patients and their families.

My mom's encounters with families always occur at a time of crisis. Usually by the time people make it to her, they've tried many other options. She does everything in her power to help, always looking for the newest, most appropriate clinical trial for each case. For as long as I can remember, she has gone to work by six a.m. and stayed at work until seven or eight p.m. She doesn't stop for lunch; she keeps a Costco-size bin of snacks in her office and will have some nuts or fruit when she feels hungry during the day.

This has always been a point of contention with my sister and me. We tell her she needs to have a lunch break, and yet it never quite happens. She always has twice the number of patients at her clinic than she should. She always puts her patients first. She is completely committed to them in their greatest moment of need. It's the thing about her that I love the most—and that worries me the most. She has spent her life caring for others, but I don't fully trust her to take care of herself.

Like my grandmother, my mom is very matter-of-fact about her future. "Your grandma is fortunate. She is very independent. There's no reason for her to go to a nursing home; she's got a clear mind, she's very active, she's got lots of interests. There are only certain activities she needs support for. She would feel isolated and depressed in a nursing home. Me, I would prefer to stay at home, too, but if I'm all by myself, it may not be a good idea because it might not be safe, unless I can have someone stay extended hours. It depends on my mental and physical capacity at the time." My mom's familiarity with the health care system and the aging process is a blessing, but I still worry that I won't be able to take care of her. I feel bad that I haven't yet given her a grandchild and that I have chosen a profession that doesn't guarantee our economic security.

"Don't worry, Ai-jen," she says with a smile. "I keep telling your cousin Sarah I'm investing in her as a nurse, so she can take care of me when I get old. No. Just kidding."

"Don't worry, Mom, we'll take care of you," I tell her. I hope my sister and I can keep that promise.

As America ages, many of us are grappling with the dignity with which our grandmothers, the suns of our universes, will live. (Because women outlive men by five to six years, by age eighty-five, there are roughly six women for every four men, and by age one hundred the ratio is more than two to one,[1] so it is, in fact, more likely to be our grandmothers' than our grandfathers' fates with which we're grappling.) There are now 5 million Americans older than eighty-five, the country's fastest-growing demographic; by 2035 that number will be 11.5 million, while 77 million baby boomers will be turning seventy. A century ago there were only 3.1 million seniors over sixty-five in the United States—one in twenty-five Americans. By 2020, it will be one in six. These are astonishing statistics.

This demographic shift, often called the "age wave," has profound implications for our economy, social system, and family life. According to the federal Administration on Aging:

The current concern about the aging of our population arises from three new conditions, linked closely to one another. The first condition is that the proportion of elderly in the total population is now substantial (13 percent). The second is that the number of elderly and the rate of aging are expected soon to increase steeply, with implications for a vast increase in the numbers of persons requiring special services (health, recreation, housing, nutrition, and the like); participating in various entitlement programs; and requiring formal and informal care. The third is a recognition of the possible implications of an aging society for the whole range of our social institutions, from education and family to business and government.

While the language of "concern" and crisis is understandable, I truly believe that the demographic shift presents us with beautiful opportunities to connect and care across generations. In the same way that the generation of people born during the baby boom made untold contributions to this country, so can the era of their retirement be a moment of teaching and transforming America. It's for this reason that I prefer to think of this demographic shift as the elder boom.

Why so many older people? Thanks to advancements in nutrition, public health, and medicine, people are living longer. In America, we gained thirty years in life expectancy during the twentieth century. Cancer is still the cause of death for about 20 percent of older Americans, and organ failure for a further 25 percent, but if you make it to age seventy-five having survived both those threats, the likelihood is that you will make it to eighty-five, even ninety-five or beyond one hundred. And it's especially in those later years, the years in which my grandmother now finds herself, that people need support. It's not just the more complex tasks, like figuring out how to open the photos of grandkids attached to e-mails or filing tax returns, but also, and mostly, the simple daily activities—cooking and eating, bathing, and safely getting around—with which many elders need assistance. They need support and care—personalized, reliable, affordable care.

Particularly in need of support is the growing population with Alzheimer's disease, currently estimated at 4.5 million Americans and expected to be four times as large by 2050. Alzheimer's is a cruel disease, frightening to imagine for oneself and devastating to watch in another. In the first two to four years of the disease, people with Alzheimer's lose short-term memories, becoming disoriented and distressed. After that, in the second phase, language and motor functions fade. They may wander and get lost even in familiar settings, and they often become suspicious, delusional, heavily depressed, and sometimes aggressive. They begin to have trouble recognizing even close family members. This often lasts two to three years, until the third phase, in which people finally lose the skills of walking, communicating, and going to the bathroom. Many live the rest of their lives in bed, unresponsive and entirely reliant on nursing care until their death.

Even in their most muted state, however, people with Alzheimer's clearly recognize and appreciate care, connection, and affection. If someone with Alzheimer's can respond to and benefit from real care, even at that late and terrifying stage when most people have written off that person, then imagine what it can do for those who still have memory, still can relate like they used to, still have so much of themselves to hold as their own, but have simply shifted from some of their younger ways of life.

The work of caring for our elders has always fallen and continues to fall primarily on the shoulders of family members. Yet our system of "informal caregiving" is straining to meet the enormous need. Many people—especially the so-called sandwich generation, the one out of every eight Americans currently juggling responsibilities for both their children and aging loved ones—are already experiencing the elder boom as a crisis. They are struggling in isolation to manage the demands for care and attention from two generations—the one that came before and the one that came after theirs—alongside work and everything else life brings. Often they do this without support for, or even acknowledgment of, the extra work, which diminishes their ability to be present and productive in other arenas of life.

This isn't to say family members shouldn't continue to provide care. There is definitely a role for traditional family caregiving—in fact, there's probably no way around some degree of family involvement given the tremendous need. Yet family members cannot possibly be relied upon to meet *all* the needs of the largest generation of older Americans ever.

Tragically, as my mother pointed out, there are also those elders who have no family upon whom they can rely for care. I think of a story I heard in New York City, told by Michael Levine, a member of an LGBT synagogue in the West Village:

"For many years I was the primary caregiver for Dick Radvin, a gay man in his seventies, and a person living at home with HIV/AIDS. I first met Dick in the 1970s when both of us served on the board of directors of our congregation. Dick was a social butterfly who seemed to know everyone in Greenwich Village and threw great dinner parties—it seemed like every week. We became fast friends and remained close through the years.

"About four or five years ago, Dick suffered a series of strokes due to the heavy medication he was taking for HIV/AIDS. After living independently in the same apartment for forty years, he was suddenly no longer able to care for himself at home, do shopping, laundry, or housecleaning. He also had difficulty making it to and from medical appointments. At this time in his life, Dick had no biological family left. On top of that, his chosen family—other New York gay men of his generation—had died of AIDS during the 1980s and 1990s.

"Our congregation was the only family Dick knew. He had worked very hard to create and sustain that network of support over the course of his life. As his closest friend, I took it on as my responsibility to care for him at the end of his life.

"I assembled a team of synagogue members to help. We shopped for him, brought food, took him to doctors, took him to social activities and walks when he could move about.

"But we slowly watched him deteriorate and lose more mobility each day until the final life-changing stroke happened. He was suddenly bedridden, unable to talk or eat, and unable to function on his own. From the hospital, he went straight to a long-term care facility, never seeing his beloved cats again, never hosting another dinner party, never again seeing the home that he'd loved for more than forty years.

"As much as Dick wanted to be cared for and to die at home, and as much as we would have wanted that for him, the last year of his life was spent in that long-term care facility. He would use his right hand, the only part of his body that still worked, to scribble with Magic Markers on a pad that he was afraid to be left alone at night. We dreaded the look on his face when we left him each day, not knowing what we would find when we returned.

"A series of episodes with pneumonia finally took his life in 2009. When it was over, we were glad to bring him to his final rest. We wish it would have been possible for him to age at home with dignity and in community."

According to one study, an estimated 1.2 million Americans over the age of sixty-five will have no living children, siblings, or spouses by 2020.[2] And I'm sad to say that not only elders without living biological relatives like Dick end their lives in isolation. In some cases, relationships between family members are too complex to be helpful, or they just fade away: out of sight, out of mind.

This disconnect between younger and elderly family members is related to a society-wide anxiety about aging. Whether it's the size of the signage used for posting important information in public spaces, the unnecessary steps at the entrances to shops that endanger people with limited mobility, or a media landscape that associates the discovery of our first gray hair or wrinkle with the end of beauty, especially for women, we receive constant messages that subtly and not so subtly diminish older people in American culture. For a 2006 global study of perceptions of beauty, the skin-care brand Dove asked women worldwide in which decade of life they thought a woman reaches the peak of her beauty. An astounding 48 percent of American women said in her twenties, whereas the majority of French, Italian, and Brazilian women said a woman is her most beautiful in her forties.[3]

A 2009 report revealed that a full 80 percent of older Americans have encountered ageist stereotypes, and between 1 million and 3 million Americans aged sixty-five or older have been injured or exploited by someone on whom they rely for care or protection.[4] Scientist and Pulitzer Prize–winning author Jared Diamond says that "older Americans are at a big disadvantage in job applications. They're at a big disadvantage in hospitals. . . . For example if only one donor heart becomes available for transplant, or if a surgeon has time to operate on only a certain number of patients, American hospitals have an explicit policy of giving preference to younger patients over older patients on the grounds that younger patients are considered more valuable to society because they have more years of life ahead of them, even though the younger patients have fewer years of valuable life experience behind them." [5]

Other cultures revere their elders, not only giving up seats for them on public transit, but also fully integrating them into all aspects of life. For example, China and other East Asian countries with a tradition of Confucianism strongly believe that with age comes elevated status, and the corresponding responsibility of younger family members to care for their elders and ancestors. In China and Korea, birthday celebrations become a much bigger deal as you turn sixty, seventy, and eighty, which is considered the pinnacle of life. The attitude is "Anyone can be young; it takes talent to be old!" Jared Diamond's research among tribal societies found many places where elders live out their lives among children, relatives, and lifelong friends. In rural Fiji, adult children even soften and pre-chew food for aging parents.

Yet in America, the fear and discomfort with which we approach aging, illness, disability, and death have had us putting older people somewhere we can't see them: in institutions. The American disability rights movement has spent decades fighting the segregation of people with disabilities in institutions, a brutal form of exclusion from society. Despite negative attention and efforts to improve the conditions in nursing homes, neglect and abuse—including rape—still occurs. People confined in institutions, especially those with dementia and other cognitive disabilities, are often physically or chemically restrained, and many are administered antipsychotics, despite the fatal danger of these drugs to people with cognitive degeneration. Malnutrition, dehydration, bedsores, dental and gum disease, and urinary tract infections occur when facilities are understaffed, which is often the case. At night, the time when many people with Alzheimer's tend to wander and require attention, many facilities have no medically certified staff available, and few staff of any kind. Conditions for workers are often awful, with substandard pay and very low status, which leads to a high rate of turnover. The majority of people institutionalized in nursing homes die within two years of their arrival.[6]

Even in the very best of such facilities, often located tens if not hundreds of miles away from elders' home communities, elders can lose their sense of belonging and connection to purpose. Thankfully, there is now widespread recognition of how broken the institutional model is. The AARP has found that 90 percent of today's older Americans want to age at home.

Not only is institutionalization undignified and unhealthy for our elders and people with disabilities; it is also *enormously* costly. In 2010, a private room in a nursing home cost $83,585 per year, on average, and the median length of stay was 29.3 months.[7] Strike the private room, and the fee for a standard stay in a shared room in a nursing home is still $50,000—and rising—per year, according to the AARP.[8] Taxpayers bear much of the cost: two-thirds of all nursing home stays are paid for by Medicaid and other government programs, with Medicaid's contribution to nursing home costs coming to $49.8 billion in 2010 (a little less than half of all Medicaid spending that year, which amounted to $117.3 billion).[9] Remember: these figures came about with a population of about 5 million over-eighty-five-year-olds. With 11.5 million elders aged eighty-five or older by the year 2035, the costs of institutionalization are unthinkable and literally unaffordable.

The best alternative keeps elders in their homes and communities as long as possible—a model that relies on the presence of unpaid family caregivers as well as professional caregivers. In recent years we've already witnessed the percentage of Medicaid devoted to nursing homes declining slightly as the demand for community-based care and home care has grown. Of course, there are still particular situations in which institutionalization cannot be avoided, but even for those requiring around-the-clock nursing or supervision, new kinds of small-group, home-like living arrangements with dedicated staff provide a much kinder and more cost-effective future than traditional nursing home facilities. A new society-wide caring infrastructure will enable us to minimize our reliance on the old and often dehumanizing institutional model.

The Unsafe Net

My grandmother is able to receive the support of Mrs. Sun because she qualifies for state-funded home care, which she supplements with the savings that she and my grandfather prepared for their old age. They were determined not to depend on their children and they knew that care could be expensive. Unfortunately, many older Americans are trapped in less fortunate situations.

Most of us pride ourselves on the contributions we make during our working years and on our intention to be independent and financially self-reliant after retirement, whether we are counting on a lifetime of workplace contributions through the government-enforced savings plan of Social Security or on our own thrift or, more likely, on a combination of both. Few of us plan to count on help from other sources. Yet very few of us have adequately planned for a long future that looks vastly different from the past or even the present. The future holds an unprecedented life span, an increasing cost of living, the largest generation ever of older adults, and increasing threats to government supports.

Right now, fewer than one-third of adults over age fifty have started saving for long-term care, one in three employed adults aged fifty-five to sixty-four has no savings for retirement, and another one-third have less than one year's salary in savings.[10] It used to be easier to save, in a more stable market, when more jobs were full-time with reliable benefit programs, when the cost of college wasn't so astronomical. Today there are many stories of elders who simply cannot get by on a monthly $1,230 ($14,760 per year) Social Security check, which the AARP confirms is the *main* source of income for almost two-thirds of older American households and the *sole* source of income for one-third.[11] Meanwhile, a home health aide costs approximately $21 per hour, paying for an assisted living facility averages $3,300 per month, and a semiprivate room in a nursing home costs $6,200 per month.[12]

According to the U.S. Census Bureau, 3.5 million seniors now live in poverty, and when health costs are factored in, the number living in poverty increases to 6.5 million. In fact, retirement is increasingly becoming a luxury. Since 1977, there has been a 172 percent increase in employment after age seventy-five. The rising costs of food and heating combined with the expense of medications and doctor's visits are requiring that everyone scrimp and save. Health costs are rising, too, and many elders are skipping doctors' visits or medications because they are too expensive.

For seniors whose primary wealth was held in their homes, the housing crash of 2008 was devastating. And the number of homeless elderly, historically almost unheard of in the United States, is rising. Based on data from the U.S. Department of Housing and Urban Development, the National Alliance to End Homelessness has predicted that among seniors "homelessness will more than double between 2010 and 2050, when over 95,000 elderly persons are projected to be homeless." Imagine two Yankee Stadiums full of elders who have worked their whole lives only to then fall through the cracks, living in shelters or underneath highway overpasses and eating in soup kitchens. These are people who contributed the larger part of a lifetime in their unique way to society, only to come to this.

Given advances in longevity, even wealthier Americans increasingly face end-of-life poverty, as a headline from a 2012 issue of *Forbes* cries out: "A Startling Reality: Your Aging Parent Runs Out of Money." In her heartbreaking book, *A Bittersweet Season*, Jane Gross, a *New York Times* columnist, shares the story of her mother's last nine years, from age seventy-nine to age eighty-eight, which she spent in living situations that became steadily more care intensive. Not counting any of her direct medical expenses, such as doctors' bills, hospital stays, surgery, or acute care (which were covered by a combination of Medicare and private insurance), the cost of her care over those nine years came to nearly $610,000. The elder Mrs. Gross's final twenty-three months, when she required round-the-clock care at a nursing home because of her inability to walk or speak, were the most expensive, at approximately $14,000 per month for a total of $320,000. Had she had cognitive impairments—from Alzheimer's, for example—her care would have been *much* more expensive.

Gross's mother was financially fortunate: she had managed to save about $470,000 through "thrift and cautious investing" for this final phase of her life. Nevertheless, in the end, she literally ran out of money and was forced to apply for Medicaid.

Jane Gross, who also created "The New Old Age" column in the *Times*, writes, "Now, as an adult child, ask yourself: Does either of your parents have a half-million dollars on hand to provide for himself or herself in old age? . . . I would guess that most of your parents don't have it, and even if they do, it may not be enough. Instead, they will need the government's help, yours—and more likely, both."

On their website, the federal Department of Health and Human Services underscores Gross's conclusion about long-term care: "With 70 percent of us needing long-term care services at some point during our lives after turning age 65, and the limited coverage of public programs, there is a good chance you will have to pay for some or all of the services out of your personal income and savings. Even if you only need a little assistance at home with personal care, paying for long-term care out of your personal income and savings can be difficult." [13]

A 2012 report from the U.S. Senate Special Committee on Aging looked at America's readiness for the elder boom, particularly for those living with Alzheimer's disease. According to the Senate report, "In the last year, [Alzheimer's] has cost $104.5 billion to Medicare services and $33.5 billion to Medicaid. . . . The

Alzheimer's Association estimates that in the next forty years, the cost of [Alzheimer's disease] to all payers, including governments, insurance companies and individuals, will total $20 trillion. The care requirements of people who struggle with the disease expand with time and endure for years." [14]

Just to put that number in perspective, the total federal budget for the United States in 2013 was $3.67 trillion—and a little less than a quarter of that, $897.19 billion, was allocated for all 2013 health and Medicare spending. Although the amount estimated on Alzheimer's spending won't be parceled out equally over those forty years, if it were calculated as an annual average, the cost per year would be $500 billion, which is more than 55 percent of our current annual spending on *all* health costs. Total spending on cancer, by way of comparison, is about $90 billion per year.

Currently America has in place a patchwork of government programs that attempt to provide assistance with income, housing, food, health care, and personal care. These are outlined in Appendix A, but if you want to skip that part, allow me to summarize here: the programs are confusing and expensive, do not provide sufficient care, and, while important in the short term absent alternatives, are ultimately outdated and inefficient.

The Old Model

Medicare is the basic health care program for those over the age of sixty-five and people with disabilities. Unfortunately, many needs of elders are not addressed by Medicare coverage. The progressive chronic conditions common to those over the age of eighty often don't get resolved with fees for service such as surgery, hospitalization, or the new technologies that Medicare privileges. Such conditions simply require ongoing attention and care. Yet, ironically, long-term care is almost never covered by Medicare, whether it is needed at home or in a facility. (*Medicaid* is the program that covers nursing home stays and sometimes home care, but only for people with disabilities and elders poor enough to qualify and is insufficient even for them. Indeed, anyone who qualifies for Medicaid benefits must remain in abject poverty in order to maintain eligibility.)

A related aspect of the problem with Medicare's fee-for-service payment model—and also the culture in which many physicians operate—is that *continuity of care* is not supported. In the ideal scenario, caring for an elder would be a team effort, with participation from and communication among a general physician, nurses, medical specialists, and other health care professionals such as psychologists, physical therapists, and nutritionists, alongside caregivers (both professional and family).

An additional challenge intensified by the elder boom is the drastically insufficient number of both registered nurses and geriatricians in the United States. A 2012 report by the *American Journal of Medical Quality* assessed the existing and impending shortage of nurses based on projected state-by-state population growth and aging populations. The researchers assigned a letter grade to every state based on the nurse shortage ratio and found "the number of states receiving a grade of 'D' or 'F' for their [registered nurses] shortage ratio will increase from 5 states in 2009, to 30 by 2030." They calculated the projected national deficit in the year 2030 at more than nine hundred thousand nurses.[15]

Meanwhile in 2013 the ratio of geriatricians to seniors over the age of eighty-five was 1:870, whereas the ideal ratio is around 1:300.[16] Given the elder boom, this ratio is set to worsen: by 2030, the nationwide ratio will drop to *one geriatrician for every 3,800 older Americans*. In her book on the shortcomings of America's end-of-life care, *Sick to Death and Not Going to Take it Anymore!*, Joanne Lynn, a geriatrician, hospice physician, and health services researcher, notes that without trained geriatricians, "illnesses in older people are misdiagnosed, overlooked or dismissed as the normal process of aging, simply because health care professionals are not trained to recognize how diseases and drugs affect older patients differently than younger patients."[17]

Basically, geriatrics is unpopular because it isn't profitable. Geriatrics is one of the lowest-paid specialties in medicine, and only 11 of America's 145 medical schools even have departments for this specialty.[18] The American Geriatrics Society calls the shortage of geriatricians a "crisis," blaming low Medicare reimbursement levels for the lack of interest in the field. Medicare reimbursements are modeled on standard procedures: a consultation that takes forty-five minutes is reimbursed at the same rate as a seven-minute visit. But examining an elder takes a long time: just getting undressed and positioned for an exam requires significant effort; adult children who come along often have many questions; and getting succinct answers to questions posed to the elder can be challenging, especially when the person has dementia or memory problems. When a doctor's visit ends, the results may not be conclusive, or may not lead to the kinds of procedures that our medical system privileges—those involving expensive technologies or specialists. As a report from the Institute of Medicine explains, "Few patients facing old age and eventually fatal chronic illnesses can count on some other essential elements of good care: for example, relief of symptoms, continuity of services and providers, a safe and functional environment, and help with planning for the future." [19]

Too often medical care for people near the end of life focuses on costly, high-tech lifesaving procedures when what is actually needed is comfort and management of ongoing conditions—also known as palliative care. At the stage where a loved one cannot be "cured" in a hospital but is not ready to die, palliative care is the only path, yet Medicare usually doesn't pay for it; instead, many elders experience regular, repeat visits to the emergency room, costing billions. It's hospital stays like these that eat up 70 percent of Medicare's budget.

A fundamental problem with our current health care system is that its measure of success is the *delay of death*, rather than the quality of life. Living with dignity, feeling comfortable, and having self-determined, steadfast loving care until the end should be our goals for health care for our elders.

Last Christmas my mother's family came together. We traveled from our different homes around the country, from New York and Houston, to Los Angeles. We gathered around a Chinese banquet with twice the number of dishes as people at the table. My mother looked relaxed, freed for a few days from the burdens of her work, and happy to have her mother and daughters around her. My aunt—whose story you will hear soon—collapsed into her chair, and everyone did their best to cheer her up and make sure no responsibilities fell on her during the family gathering.

After eating, we played mah-jong. With the colorful tiles

spread on the table in front of her, my grandmother emerged in full force, in all her glory as a patient teacher, an edgy truth teller, a strategic pragmatist, and a winner, while laughing the entire time. The sound of the tiles clicking against one another was familiar and soothing for all of us.

"I'm at peace with whatever may come," she said contentedly.

We must take action now to plan for our grandparents' futures as well as our own futures. When we really examine the scope and scale of the coming elder boom, we won't have a choice but to make care a priority. Everyone will be touched by this change in the American demographic. We're going to have to rethink everything—how we live, work, and play, and especially how we organize our family and community life: how we take care of each other across generations. The public and the private realms of life will necessarily come together in new ways, because none of us will be able to find solutions alone. This process of establishing the necessary infrastructure for care will create significant economic opportunity.

In the caring new world we must create, our grandparents will have healthy, life-sustaining options: the personalized support and care they need to live life on their terms. As we will see, this will also necessarily mean that caregivers like Mrs. Sun receive the wages, benefits, and supports they need to support their families, prepare for their own futures, and provide quality care to the individuals and families they support.

We can view the elder boom as an opportunity to respond from the basis of something that all of us across the political spectrum hold dear: our right to live with dignity, independence, and self-determination. From that place, we can work together to reorganize society so that in all phases of life we can count on love, connection, and care. What could feel like the beginning of an epic national crisis in care can in fact be one of our greatest opportunities for positive transformation at every level.

Mrs. Sun and my grandmother often cook together in my grandmother's kitchen. Or Mrs. Sun will bring cooked food that she has made at home in her own kitchen. My grandmother is quite a cook herself, always learning and trying new dishes. They share their secrets with one another; both of our families benefit from their kitchen collaborations. PHOTOGRAPH BY MICHELE ASSELIN

2

THE SANDWICH GENERATION

> There are only four kinds of people in the world:
> those who have been caregivers,
> those who are currently caregivers,
> those who will be caregivers,
> and those who need caregiving.
>
> —Rosalynn Carter

If you're like me, you don't want to think about your parents becoming frail. When we hear about someone else's elderly parent needing outside care or extra help, we think quietly, *I'd take care of my mother myself. I wouldn't leave her in the hands of some stranger. If it comes to that, that's what I would do.* Well, the odds are that it will come to that, as I explained in the previous chapter, thanks to medical advancements that are keeping older people alive but rarely self-reliant well into their eighties and nineties.

Most of us believe that providing care for our parents ourselves is the right thing to do; that it is what is expected of us; that it's only fair given how our parents took care of us when we were children. Our ethnic, cultural, and religious backgrounds play a part in this, instilling deep messages about filial obligation: honor thy mother and father. Daughters tend to feel this responsibility most of all.

What I hope to make clear in this chapter is that taking full responsibility for the care of an aging relative is—contrary to truly well-intentioned beliefs—not necessarily a real option, or the best option for many families. As journalist and author Gail Sheehy writes in *Passages in Caregiving*, "The secret of caregiving success [is] . . . we cannot do it alone. No one can. We must create a support circle—a circle of care." [1] Please don't misunderstand me: adult children absolutely need to stay involved in their aging parents' lives, but times have changed. Today's middle-aged children of elder parents are often too far away or too busy to provide more than money (if they can afford that). Of course, money is a big piece of the equation. Yet above all, providing years of increasingly comprehensive support for someone struggling with a chronic condition is a massive job. It's a job for a professional. From the growing body of literature about family caregiving, it's becoming clear that the integrity and quality of family relationships endure best when families can enlist support from professionals.

I'm fortunate that my own parents don't yet need care. But like most Americans, I didn't have to look far to find someone who is providing care for a parent, while also being a parent, holding a full-time job, and being a partner: my aunt, the wife of my mom's younger brother.

Every weekend for the past five years, my aunt has rushed from her commuter job as a computer programmer in Thousand Oaks to care for her ninety-five-year-old mother in Los Angeles. "I have to keep an eye on her all the time. I feel too nervous to even go to the bathroom and have her out of my sight for that long. Anything can happen."

My aunt also has a daughter, my cousin Sarah, who's studying to be a nurse. Sarah was still living at home when my aunt began spending every weekend taking care of her mother, although now that Sarah's in her early twenties, she's living on her own. While Sarah's increased independence lessened the pressure on her mother somewhat, my aunt still carries around guilt for not being able to do it all. When she arrives at our family gatherings, she is exhausted—physically, mentally, and emotionally. Yet she can't scale back at her job to work less than full-time because she needs the health insurance.

Mother, full-time employee, caregiver, and caregiver's employer: my aunt (who prefers to remain unnamed) has been juggling these responsibilities since 2007, when her father passed away. A year after that, she recalls, "My mother had a really bad fall and a piece of her spinal cord fractured, and she was bedridden for a couple months. That was when her health really deteriorated. She cannot walk too far and has to sit down a lot. And she became incontinent. Now she has to wear diapers.

"At first, we hired a part-time caregiver to work with her in the morning. The caregiver bought groceries, helped with errands, did a little cleaning, took my mother to some appointments, prepared lunch, and then left. But then my mother's memory started to go. Once she forgot to turn off the stove, burned the pot, and set off the smoke alarm without realizing what happened. Another time she left the water running, the sink overflowed, and the whole room flooded. Then she fell when no one was around, and she couldn't get up. She managed to crawl to the phone to call for help.

"That was when we knew we had to hire someone full-time. So three years ago we hired a live-in caregiver to be with her twenty-four hours a day, five days a week. I'm a little worried because my mom is becoming a little paranoid and doesn't trust the caregiver. She always thinks that the caregiver stole her things. A couple of times she told me her caregiver stole her jewelry or her money; then she finds it later.

"On weekends it's my turn. I keep asking my sister to move closer to us. But she has her own problems and cannot do a lot of things. She's doing her best. She still calls my mom every day."

This scenario with my aunt mirrors the most common situation in families across America. The bulk of the work falls on the shoulders of one sibling, more often a daughter than a son. Women make up two-thirds of today's caregivers.[2] The average caregiver for an older adult is a fifty-year-old woman who provides nineteen hours of care per week—essentially a part-time job—for an average of four years. Even when other relatives are involved in the care, they generally do less than 10 percent of the work.

Supporting someone with the activities of daily life—bathing, dressing, walking, cooking, eating, housekeeping, shopping, transportation to appointments—may not sound like such a big deal, but with a frail or confused elderly person or someone with any number of chronic illnesses, any one of these tasks can be extremely time-consuming. In the spectrum of attitudes from easygoing to impossible, my aunt's mom is somewhere in the middle. Nevertheless, my aunt says it takes her pretty much the whole day to help her mother bathe and get dressed, prepare and eat meals, go out for a walk, and take trips to the bathroom: "Going to the bathroom is a big production; each trip runs about fifteen minutes. She has a history of bladder infections so I keep asking her to drink more water. But if you drink more water you have to go to the bathroom more. She keeps saying she wants to cut down her trips to the bathroom because it's such an ordeal. But if she doesn't go she'll get another bladder infection.

"She insists that she can change her own diaper, but it's very hard. You know Chinese older ladies—they wear a lot of layers! She wears the diaper, thermals, pants, and a big belt—like a waist supporter. There's a Velcro thing on the waist supporter that you have to use a lot of strength to have it reach. She always insists she can do it on her own but it's just too difficult."

My aunt also handles her mother's finances, fills out the mind-bogglingly complex government assistance forms, and manages the paid caregiver. In-home Supportive Services of California covers eighty-two hours of her mother's care per month, at $9 per hour. The rest of the twenty-four-hour care is paid for by my aunt and her two siblings. "My mother also has a small savings, which she doesn't want to spend. But I manage her money, and I spend some of it on her care. She doesn't know; I don't tell her because she wants to leave it to us. She constantly complains that she doesn't want a caregiver and that she's capable of caring for herself. I told her it's only going to get worse; it's not going to get better. It's cruel to say that; I shouldn't say that.

"Sometimes when I take care of my mom, I curse. I'm just mentally and physically so tired. I don't have anyone to talk to. I don't want to keep whining to people about how tired I am. Keep it to yourself, okay? I don't want them to know. I'm okay. I cry to myself, and then I'm fine.

"A lot of people who used to be my friends are no longer my

friends because I cannot join them for lunch or do fun things with them; that makes me sad, too. Strange to have friends who are only with you during happy times, not times of need. There are not that many people who will really listen to you in a time of need. And some make me feel like I'm just complaining all the time. I try not to talk about my problems too much; I don't want people to hear me whining.

"I keep praying, 'Give me more patience, give me more love.' I know this is only temporary."

My aunt is really hard on herself when she catches herself thinking about the inevitable moment when her mother passes on and no longer needs care. In fact, spoken or unspoken, a desire for the elder or sick relative to die is incredibly common among family caregivers. A woman in an online support forum for caregivers anonymously shared: "I know it's horrible but there have been times when I wished that my dad would pass away so all of this would stop. My nightly prayer consists of, 'Please make it stop. Please make it stop. Please make it stop.'" Caregivers who speak openly about these feelings actually provide comfort for the many who carry terrible guilt about thinking and feeling similarly. When I talk to my aunt, I tell her that to crave resolution and to want to put this difficult chapter behind her does not make her a bad daughter or a bad person. It comes with the territory of her position; she is like so many others who have disproportionate responsibilities to provide care without adequate moral support, financial support, or acknowledgment. For me, the deeper question is really this: what does it mean when caregivers feel so unsupported, desperate, and alone in this work that they dwell on thoughts of the death of their beloved family members because they cannot imagine sustaining the necessary care?

As grueling as my aunt's situation is, it pales in comparison to many of the stories I've heard from family caregivers. After all, my aunt has managed to keep her job, is able to hire professional caregivers for her mother, even receiving some support to do so from the state of California, and must only—*only!*—do that work herself on the weekends. Millions of Americans are less fortunate than she is. A man from Florida who asked to remain anonymous fumes about the failure of the system to support his doing the right thing: "I just got off the phone with Florida Unemployment and they are saying that because I chose to leave my job to take care of my parents, I will not get unemployment. My parents are in their eighties and very sick, my Dad in final-stage Parkinson's, and heart problems and a lot more for my mom. God bless them and I love them, but I don't know how much longer I can take this. They have very little income left. They do get Social Security (not Supplemental Security Income). They have Medicare but are just over [the income cutoff] so are not able to get assistance from Medicaid. They have no one else to care for them and can't afford to pay someone to do it.

"Does the government want to pay for my parents to go into a nursing home that costs about $50,000 yearly or more? Then we all end up paying through our taxes. They should do the math! Why can't the government step in to pay me the small amount of extension of unemployment, so I can keep my parents happy by letting them stay at home? Why can't they at least give us health insurance while we are taking care of our parents?

"I am scared to death of what I am going to do financially. *Yes*, it was my choice. I gave up everything to do this and I am being damned for being a good son and caregiver. I was making good money up north and gave it all up, including my home, to take care of my parents. I feel I am being punished for helping the most important people in my life. What is wrong with this system? The system sucks. No wonder the adult kids aren't able to take care of their parents. They can't afford it. *Sad!* I have nothing left. I'm not proud to admit I cry a lot lately, a grown man crying."

Some family caregivers choose to leave their jobs; others are let go. Caregiver Celia Watson Seupel, a regular contributor to the "New Old Age" column of the *New York Times*, writes about getting fired from her job when caring for her mother, who's in her nineties and has vascular dementia, became too distracting:

It's easy for others to say "Hire a caregiver," or "Quit your job." We could afford neither. My mother's savings were exhausted, and I was in debt. My husband and I were separated, and he was disabled, unable to contribute. My father and my siblings were dead. Even with my job, it seemed I could never pay all the bills. And we were digging into a home-equity line of credit. . . .

I did hire a very part-time caregiver who wanted more money per hour than I made. My mother hated her. While I searched for someone else, I tried bringing my mother to work with me. She sat in the conference room reading while I worked in my three-person office. Every hour my mother would step into my office and inquire, with increasingly strained civility, when we would be going home. We left at lunchtime.

I toured the only local senior day care center. It was hideous: smelly, somnambulant and depressing. My mother was too vital for such a place.

In the end, it was a blessing that I was fired. I was forgetting appointments, making mistakes and miserable. . . . It wasn't until I got fired that Mom started to relax.[3]

Even for those fortunate enough to have parents with sufficient savings and private insurance that covers caregiving and supported living, the pressure is enormous. I spoke with a colleague of mine at Caring Across Generations named Robin, the mother of now eighteen- and twenty-one-year-old sons, who has managed the care of her parents for more than a decade. Her father has Parkinson's disease, and her mother had breast cancer for eighteen years, which metastasized to her brain before she passed away a few years ago. When we talked, Robin's main responsibilities were her father's finances and medications, because he lives in a senior apartment building with assistance where two meals per day are provided and can rely on the support of paid caregivers during the day.

Robin told me, "Between a pension and long-term care insurance, finances are okay so far. We're lucky that way. His long-term care insurance pays for twelve hours of support from home aides per day, but this still means he's alone at night. So he wakes up in the middle of the night and can't get to the bathroom. His cognitive functions keep deteriorating, and now he needs help standing up from a chair.

"Live-in, twenty-four-hour support would make much more sense, but that's not provided through the agency, and the long-term care insurance mandates hiring care workers through an agency. Rather than one aide who might become more trusted, there's a rotating cast of at least five characters. It's not the same level of companionship. One person was caught stealing from him.

"He mostly manages and directs the workers himself, but if there's a big problem, I have to communicate to the agency and they communicate to the workers. It seems like we need a better system for reporting and communicating.

"I do my best to let him be independent and make decisions for himself. But there are things where I can't let him decide: it would be dangerous. The hardest part is watching this brilliant man, a former chemical engineer and then a lawyer for the Justice Department, lose his cognitive abilities. It's so easy to get mad at him, but it's not his fault.

"My kids are amazing, but not amazing enough to step up and really help care for their grandfather. It's hard for them that he's not who he used to be. Sometimes it feels like everyone needs your emotional energy. Everywhere you turn someone needs to tell you their problem and there's no peaceful space."

No matter their level of income or education, no matter the size of their family or the region in which they live, adult children of aging parents often describe these same emotions—feeling torn, trapped, stressed, sad, resentful, and even furious. In her self-described rant in *The Atlantic*, Los Angeles–based writer and actor Sandra Tsing Loh rages:

He is taking everything! He is taking all the money. He's taken years of my life (sitting in doctors' offices, in pharmacies, in waiting rooms). With his horrid, selfish, grotesque behavior, he's chewed through every shred of my sentimental affection for him. He's taken the serenity I fought for—and won—in 1,000 hours of therapy centered on my family. In fact, he's destroyed my belief in "family" as a thing that buoys one up. . . . That's right: my family is throwing all our money away on powdering our 91-year-old dad's giant-baby ass, leaving nothing for my sweet little daughters, with their thoughts of unicorns and poetry and dance, my helpless little daughters. . . .[4]

These stories only scratch the surface of the vast sea of experiences of 43.5 million Americans providing care for an elder family member. Of them, 20 million[5] are struggling in the sandwich generation: squeezed, pulled, and torn between the demands of their children and the needs of their parents. As the number of Americans aged sixty-five or over mushrooms from about 42 million today to 71 million by 2030, the pressure on middle-aged children will become untenable. Today's sandwich generation is made up of the younger baby boomers, who were the largest ever generation in America's history before the Millennials. By 2030, tomorrow's sandwich generation—my peers and I—will be taking care of the baby boomers, who, born between 1946 and 1964, will have reached their seventies and eighties by 2030. We are increasingly spending more years caring for our parents than for our children, in part because many couples often have more parents (four between them) than offspring (in families with children, the average number of children is 1.86) who need care.

As more women have had and continue to have children later, between their late thirties and midforties, children are often still at home, needing care, when health issues arise with seventy-something or older parents. The later-in-life mothers and fathers may have expected to work an extra ten to fifteen years after retirement age to finance their kids' university educations, but they did not foresee how much a decade of care for their dependent parents would cost. In their prime years of professional capacity and earning power, they may not be able to set anything aside for their own senior years and worry about burdening their offspring in turn.

My aunt, for example, is intimately familiar with the fact that government programs are already falling short: what will they look like in twenty-five or thirty years, she wonders, and how will she manage when she reaches her mother's age? "I don't want Sarah to have to do the same thing I'm doing now. I don't want to be her burden when I get old. I don't think it's fair to her. But I don't think I'll be as lucky as my mom's generation to have a full-time person to take care of me. I don't think we will be able to afford that when I get to that age."

A number of factors intensify the situation of family members caring for elders. While child care receives more widespread recognition (though arguably still not enough), and at least limited support from employers and government programs, eldercare is less acknowledged in our society. And child care is different from eldercare. Except for the occasional broken leg or other emergency, most care for a child without significant disabilities follows school hours and vacation calendars; it generally spans the sixteen to eighteen years from birth to college or moving out.

Eldercare is much more erratic: strokes and heart attacks, falls and other accidents caused by frail bodies and failing memories— they can happen at any time, and do. When an emergency does occur, many family members assume the elder will need their support for a while until things are back to normal, only to find that the need usually carries on, and intensifies, over *years* instead of weeks or months. Above all, at the end of each path generally lie opposite outcomes: your care for your children will have, you hope, launched them into a healthy, fulfilling, joyful life ahead. For an elder, even a path through a rich and dignified old age will inevitably end in death, and the emotional and spiritual work of preparing for death is part of the difficulty.

Because we are such a mobile society, adult children often live far away from their parents. It's not just children doing the moving, either: many better-off sixty-five-year-olds move to sunny senior communities in Florida, Arizona, or California immediately following retirement, while they are still active and healthy. Then, when they grow older and need more care and support, they are often far away from their adult children. If they can financially and physically afford to, they sometimes choose to move back, in what's known as reverse migration. While bringing them closer to their children, this reverse migration can trigger unfortunate consequences for elders' relationships with retirement-age friends and—importantly—with doctors. Finding a new doctor at the age of seventy-five or eighty is challenging if not impossible.

Other trends impact the state of family caregiving as well. Because the average American family has steadily shrunk over the last century, there are fewer siblings and relatives with whom to share eldercare. The economic downturn over the last decade has been particularly hard on elders, who hold most of their wealth in suddenly diminishing home values and investments, while the costs of health care, food, gas, and the like have increased. On top of that, because unemployment has worsened, more and more twentysomething offspring, the so-called boomerangers, are returning home and needing support from parents who are in their fifties and sixties—the same parents whose eighty- and ninetysomething parents require care.

From Superhero to Super Friends

Caring for an elderly family member involves such a wide range of skills and expertise that only a superhuman person could do this work alone. Really—it is virtually impossible for one person to master the job, which can include everything from lifting a frail body in and out of bed; administering a long and frequently changing list of medications in varying doses at varying times of day; cleaning and applying ointment to wounds or sores; filling out twenty-page government assistance forms; managing bank accounts, bills, investments, and legal documents; running interference with doctors, therapists, aides, insurance agents, and staff at residential facilities; and facilitating opportunities to enjoy a full life with family and in community. Yet tens of millions of Americans—and millions more in the years to come—are each individually called on to juggle all of these tasks.

One of the first areas in which family caregivers quickly need to become expert is the elder family member's medical condition—or, as is often the case, multiple conditions. This can involve calling or visiting doctors, as well as researching independently to get the whole picture, including the pros and cons involved in various treatments and what to expect in the future. It also means negotiating with elders, making sure their needs and personal choices are taken into account, and balancing self-determination with medical protocols and recommendations.

The next area of expertise for caregivers to learn is insurance and government programs. Public support for the elderly is a morass of programs administered by many different agencies at the city, county, state, and federal levels. Government support of elders is overwhelmingly confusing and tragically fragmented.

Even the experts can't keep all these programs straight. Good luck being the harried daughter of an aging mother or a mother with a disability whose resources are running out.

Is the elder enrolled in Medicare, and if so, which parts? Is she eligible for Medicaid? How does Medicaid function where the elder lives, since it varies widely from state to state? Medicaid applications are long and rigorous, requiring copies of all kinds of certificates and policies that even the most organized among us would be hard-pressed to pull together. Eldercare lawyers charge thousands of dollars to handle them, as much as $10,000 in some places.

What is covered by any insurance programs in place? Does the elder have private long-term care insurance? Most long-term care policies cover a portion of residential care in an assisted living residence or a nursing home. Some also pay for services at home or in the community, such as home care and adult day care services. There are also programs and assistance available from nongovernment sources, such as churches, synagogues, nonprofit organizations, or support groups for a specific disease, which family caregivers can research—in the unlikely event of a spare moment.

Additionally, family caregivers often must manage an elder's legal and financial matters. They may take the role of power of attorney, to handle financial matters, or health care proxy, to be in charge of making medical decisions when the elder cannot. They might need to set up an advance directive, or living will, which informs health care professionals what kinds of care the elder wants and does not want if he or she cannot participate in a discussion, including do-not-resuscitate orders. Every state has different rules about advance directives. These are complex ethical responsibilities: just broaching these subjects with an aging parent and the rest of the family can be difficult, time-consuming, and painful. If there are assets such as real estate and the elder has yet to draw up a will, finding a lawyer to create the will also can fall on the caregiver's shoulders.

While a family with multiple siblings means these tasks can be shared, one sibling usually needs to assume the role of leader and central organizer, which is a job unto itself. Family meetings may need to be held; information about medical, legal, logistical, and financial options must be communicated; final tie-breaking decisions need to be made. Experts advise that one sibling be the point person for all doctors and health care providers, to minimize confusion and streamline the unavoidable complexity.

Finally, at the foundation of all these responsibilities is the most intensive and continuous work: the activities of daily life. This includes bathing, dressing, walking, cooking, eating, housekeeping, shopping, transportation, conversation, and companionship. In polls, family caregivers say that the most challenging tasks of all are managing incontinence—the first time your parent needs a diaper will probably feel like the world is imploding—as well as tending to wounds and administering complex medication schedules. Activities of daily life are time-consuming and demanding, well suited for handing over to a trained care professional, so that the family can focus on medical, ethical, legal, and financial issues. They are also among the most important parts of caregiving, countering isolation and supporting people to live full lives within their community.

All in all, the value of the work that family caregivers provide is in the hundreds of billions of dollars. A recent study by the National Alliance for Caregiving and AARP found that

44.4 million Americans are providing unpaid care; if we had to pay for this care, it would cost us approximately $375 billion per year—more than three times as much as government spending on caregiving.[6] A report in the *Monthly Labor Review* focused just on the contributions of sandwich generation women between the ages of forty-five and fifty-six: "On average, they spend $10,000 and 1,350 hours each year helping their children and parents. For the economy as a whole, these women represent important resource flows. With roughly 20 million American women in this age group . . . [this is] on the order of $18 billion and 2.4 billion hours each year."[7] Alzheimer's disease presents its own unique—and growing—set of costs and responsibilities for families. The Alzheimer's Association estimates that the work of the 15 million Americans providing unpaid care for family members with Alzheimer's disease or dementia was valued at $210 billion in 2010.[8]

While I don't read comic books myself, my friends who are avid comic book fans tell me that early Superman stories focused on Superman saving the day on his own. Later stories, however, shifted to the Super Friends and the Justice League. These stories depicted Superman as one, perhaps the leader, but just one of a large team of people, all of whose special powers are needed. We need a Super Friends approach to caregiving. Imagine a nation of Caring Super Friends, teams of people who support one another in the caregiving process, breaking the isolation that has come to define the family caregiver experience, once and for all.

At What Cost

As former senator and secretary of state Hillary Clinton recently argued, "Just because family caregiving is unpaid does not mean it is costless."[9] Physically strenuous, emotionally exhausting, socially isolating, and spiritually demanding: of course this work takes its toll. Doubts, unresolved questions, and insecurities plague my aunt and millions of other family caregivers:

- How do I divide my time and attention among my children, parent, and partner?
- How do I prioritize? How do I choose between paying for my child's college education and paying for my parent's care, let alone saving for my own future?
- How do I make time for my marriage, relationships, and friendships?
- How do I make time for myself? Will I ever be able to take a vacation again?
- How do I relieve my isolation, especially when all I want to do with an hour that opens up is to be alone?
- How do I find the financial resources to provide for everyone?
- How do I balance my work and career goals with family care responsibilities?
- How do I manage the constant guilt of not meeting my own and everyone else's expectations?
- Do I just accept that I can't do anything well?
- Am I the worst daughter/son ever, for wishing my aging parent would just die, for not having been available that fateful day, for not visiting more often . . . ?

Studies show that family caregivers, especially those who must balance jobs with unpaid caregiving, are likely to neglect themselves to the detriment of their health. Sleep deprivation, stress, depression, immune system deficiency, diabetes, and hypertension are common.[10] According to the American Psychological Association's 2007 Stress in America survey, women in the sandwich generation aged thirty-five to fifty-four feel more stress than any other age group. In a 2013 AARP poll, one in five family caregivers says her or his life has gotten worse since assuming caregiving duties, with less happiness, less satisfaction with social life, less exercise, and weight gain.[11] Alzheimer's caregivers report even higher levels of physical strain and emotional stress.[12] As you'd expect, the more responsibilities she or he must manage, the more devastating the impact on the caregiver's quality of life. Those who perform five or more tasks reported:

- feeling stressed from juggling caregiving and other responsibilities (75 percent);
- having no time to themselves (70 percent);
- feeling they were on constant watch (53 percent);
- being depressed in the past two weeks (52 percent);
- feeling stressed from talking to too many providers (47 percent); and
- worrying that they would make a mistake (40 percent).[13]

Research also shows that caring for aging parents shared among siblings often causes childhood family dynamics to reignite, old wounds to reopen, and the healing of family therapy to come undone. Even though it streamlines and simplifies caregiving and is therefore considered advisable for one family member to take on the role of primary caregiver, this responsibility is not carried without resentment. Old childhood labels—who was always "the responsible one" and who was the "the unreliable one"?—often resurface. In her book *They're Your Parents Too! How Siblings Can Survive Their Parents' Aging Without Driving Each Other Crazy*, Francine Russo tells the story of the Kellers, a typical family: "Before they reassembled to deal with their increasingly frail mother, they had all gone different ways. There were marriages, divorces, remarriages, kids, and grandkids. By the time Dottie moved back to their hometown, twice-divorced and still a dreamy romantic, her younger sister Arlene had become a player in their town, a trusted financial advisor and confident leader. As Dottie found out, being older didn't count for much any more. . . . As they confronted their mother's new dependency, and glimpsed her mortality, they found themselves acting out of old needs, reenacting old rivalries." [14] A number of studies with titles like "Redressing Inequity in Parent Care Among Siblings" and "Mothers' Favoritism in Later Life" have found the greatest source of stress for family caregivers to be not the parent but sibling disagreements. [15]

And there is a unquestionably a gender divide in family caregiving: daughters are still doing the lion's share, though the participation of sons is on the rise—to 33 percent of family caregivers in 2009. [16] The division of labor is gendered, too: a sister usually bears responsibility for the most intimate of tasks, such as changing diapers, cleaning wounds, and bathing—duties seen as less desirable or more "messy"—while a brother is more likely to pay bills, handle lawyers, and find suitable technology to support the parent.

One beleaguered woman explained in an online support group the dynamics involved in her brother taking over responsibility for her father's care when she couldn't carry on:

I was running on pure adrenaline, pure stress, when it was brought to my attention that I had not turned in a form I was supposed to turn in a month prior. This was a mistake of epic proportions and is costing us dearly. This was also the turning point when I realized that I couldn't do it any longer. I couldn't continue to be caregiver and advocate and mother and employee. I broke down on the phone with my brother and he stepped in. . . .

I've become so depressed and so down on myself because of the mistake I made. I made it right, . . . and we're ok now (I hope) but I can't forgive myself. Everything I had shared with my brother up until that time is now questioned. My brother gets different answers than the ones I gave him and this infuriates me. I know what I've been told and it's not like I pulled information out of the air but the information my brother gets is different than the information I got. But my credibility is shot. I know for certain what the [doctor] told me however [the doctor] told my brother something completely different, and because of this huge mistake I made it looks like I'm the one getting the information wrong but I'm not. I understood the [doctor] perfectly. . . .

It's affected my relationship with my daughter. It'll probably be the end of my relationship with my brother.[17]

In one of the most heatedly commented upon posts on her "New Old Age" blog, Jane Gross quoted a geriatric case manager named Marsha Foley who advised sisters to accept this division of labor: " 'part of why women get so mad' at their brothers 'is because they're not suffering enough.' [Brothers] compartmentalize better, do what needs to be done and then get on with their day. They rarely indulge in woulda-coulda-shouldas. And if they can delegate or pay for what mom or dad needs, they're satisfied that they've done their part." [18] While we definitely need to continue to change the culture around expectations of daughters, most geriatric experts agree that sibling rivalry and fights for gender equality inside families should be put aside to allow everyone to focus on the parent needing care.

Providing care for an elderly family member has impacts not just on mental, emotional, and physical well-being; it also carries a heavy financial burden. In order to provide care, most family caregivers must rearrange their work schedules, reduce their hours, or take unpaid leaves of absence. Some find they must turn down opportunities for overtime or promotions or travel. Some use sick leave or vacation time.

According to the most recent edition of *Caregiving in the United States*, a full 70 percent of caregivers report making changes such as cutting back on their working hours, changing jobs, stopping work entirely, taking a leave of absence, or other such changes as a result of their caregiving role. Female caregivers are more likely than males to make certain work arrangements: reducing hours or taking a less demanding job (16 percent for women vs. 6 percent for men), giving up work entirely (12 percent vs. 3 percent), and losing job benefits (7 percent vs. 3 percent).[19]

Other countries offer family caregivers support in the form of payment, respite, and tax breaks; for example, Germany's mandatory public long-term care insurance offers the choice of a cash payout, which can be used to pay family caregivers. Not so in the United States. Granted, the Family and Medical Leave Act makes possible flexible work arrangements or unpaid leave for people who are caring for family members and allows pretax dollars to be set aside for eldercare expenses. However, not many employers provide this option. In fact, while three-quarters of employers offer child care assistance, only one-third offer eldercare assistance.[20] Larger companies (50 percent of them, according to one 2003 study[21]) have been more likely than small and midsize firms (22 percent of them, in 2007[22]) to offer this help. The disparity between the availability of support for child care and that for eldercare is pretty astounding, given that everyone has parents and grandparents, but not everyone has children.

Taking time off or accessing other kinds of support from your employer for eldercare is a mark of privilege, too: people in less secure, lower-paid jobs rarely have this kind of flexibility or autonomy. It's out of the question for them to take off work to deal with a family emergency. The *Caregiving in the United States 2009* report found that "caregivers in households with less than $50,000 in income are twice as likely as those in higher income households to report a high degree of financial hardship as a result of caring for their loved one."[23]

Some family caregivers, as we've heard, have to leave their jobs entirely. These kinds of sacrifices—which result in a temporary loss of income, loss of retirement income or other benefits, or lost opportunities for career advancement—create a domino effect, hurting the caregiver's children and other family members, not to mention society and the economy as a whole. According to a 2010 report, a family caregiver can expect a loss of productivity both at work (on average an 18.5 percent reduction in productivity) and in daily life (a 27 percent reduction in productivity).[24] Someone who takes time off from work to provide care for an aging parent will lose more than $300,000 in wages and benefits over a lifetime, according to the AARP: men will lose $283,716 and women will lose $324,044. For American businesses, the estimated loss of productivity from full-time employed caregivers comes to a staggering $33.6 billion per year.[25]

Then there are the actual costs of care borne by families either in addition to, or in place of, public support or private insurance. While well-off families can often pay for the cost of housing, help, and medical care themselves, and very poor families have access to Medicaid and other programs, in between there are the millions of working poor families and the millions more with low to moderate incomes who don't qualify for assistance but also can't afford the costs of eldercare.

Plus there are a lot of costs involved that no government program and no private insurance will cover. Jane Gross writes that she and her brother "spent thousands upon thousands supplementing her [mother's] expenses in assisted living, buying her both essentials (groceries, clothes, furniture) and luxuries (books, restaurant meals, a VCR), hiring private-duty home health aides when she was in the nursing home and staffing was poor on holiday weekends, and getting her a motorized wheelchair and a certain assisted speaking device when strokes impacted her ability to walk and talk. None of this was covered by Medicare, by Medicaid, or by her long-term care insurance policy; none of it was considered a tax deduction for either of us on our tax returns." In 2012, families of people with Alzheimer's spent an estimated $33 billion in out-of-pocket costs.

There is no question we are failing today's American families. Our current system is a holdover from another time, when life expectancy was around sixty years and dementia was rare. It's from a time when society relied on the uncompensated work of women who didn't hold jobs outside the home. It's from a time when the national ratio of elderly to young workers was radically different, making for a more balanced inflow and outflow of government dollars for social programs.

Looking at the total landscape of our economy, it's clear that the system cannot hold if so many adults between the ages of thirty-five and sixty, traditionally considered the peak of a person's productive capacity, are stretched so thin. To assume that today's middle-aged Americans will bear not only the financial but also the psychological and physical costs of caring for the largest generation of elders ever is untenable. Those of us who are childless are even more at a loss when we contemplate our later years, wondering who will do for us what we do for our parents.

Everyone I talk to says the same thing: this doesn't make any sense, it doesn't work for anyone, and many people are at the brink of their capacity to live in this upside-down world. Some people are lucky, others have found creative ways to take control of their situation and make it the best it can be, and yet others are trying to take control of the system overall—or elements of it—by fighting for the changes they need and they know we all need. We desperately need a system overhaul to create a twenty-first-century infrastructure to ensure dignity and independence for Americans of all ages and circumstances. And that desperation is driving scores of people I meet every day to take action.

The Lasting Value

While the elder boom translates to a number of grave challenges for family caregivers, and for the sandwich generation in particular, it's important to understand that the impacts of providing eldercare are not all negative, not by a long shot. Alongside words like "grueling," "isolating," and "exhausting," I hear things like "rewarding," "life-affirming," and "healing." In *Passages in Caregiving*, one of the best resources available for family caregivers, Gail Sheehy writes, "The chance to give back some of the love and compassion and tender care to the parents who were there for us . . . is a gift. Often the caregiving commitment can bring a loosely-knit family closer together, as long as each member is made to feel valuable for his or her unique contribution." Many family caregivers say that if they had to do it again, they'd make the same choices, even if it meant leaving or losing a job, taking a cut in income, and missing out on time with their friends. Once their parent has passed away, most family caregivers say they have no regrets and that what they learned from their parents about aging and dying with dignity are the most important lessons they've ever received.

I love the quote from former first lady Rosalynn Carter that opens this chapter. It's a reminder that every single one of us has experienced caregiving at some point in our lives, at a minimum when we were infants or when we got sick. It also reminds us that each of us has the potential to be a caregiver in every moment. Even if you are in the position of having neither children nor aging parents who are dependent on you, you can still choose to provide care for someone else, even if it's a stranger at the store or on public transit. The more we practice being allies to seniors, people with disabilities, and those members of our communities who rely on personal assistance and care both in and outside the home, the more fully human we will all become.

Care is perhaps the most powerful expression of our human

interdependence. In the context of caring relationships, we are never simply giving or receiving; it's always both. The more we embrace the role of caregiver ourselves, and the more we affirm the experience of depending on others in order to get our own needs met, the clearer our realization will become of how vital care work is. The more we recognize the value of seniors, people with disabilities, and others who build rich and satisfying lives through extended networks of personal assistance and care, the more skilled we will become at structuring interdependence into our everyday lives. I believe this realization will ultimately shift our culture toward fully accounting for the work of caring and will help shape our policies and social programs to support families across generations.

In the end, every generation is a generation sandwiched between two others. But the "sandwich generation" moniker has arisen now, today, because care work has never been more necessary and at the same time more elusive, incomplete, and life changing (for better or worse) than it is now. Therefore, the greatest contribution this generation may make, aside from birthing the Internet, may be birthing a new system that distributes care across generations in a way we all want, need, and deserve.

The physical embrace, while less common historically in Chinese culture than in others, has delightfully become more and more a part of our family culture. I am discovering that there are many simple things in life that we can offer one another—a touch, kindness, a warm smile—that hold the potential to change everything. The end of the Alice Walker poem "We Alone," which I first read in Gloria Steinem's book *Moving Beyond Words* captures it beautifully:

> This could be our revolution.
> To love what is plentiful
> As much as what is scarce.

PHOTOGRAPH BY MICHELE ASSELIN

3

THE CARING PROFESSIONALS

All work is empty save when there is love. . . . And what is it to work with love? It is to weave the cloth with threads drawn from your heart, even as if your beloved were to wear that cloth. It is to build a house with affection, even as if your beloved were to dwell in that house. It is to sow seeds with tenderness and reap the harvest with joy, even as if your beloved were to eat the fruit. It is to charge all things you fashion with a breath of your own spirit, and to know that all the blessed dead are standing about you and watching.

—Kahlil Gibran, *The Prophet*

Family caregivers clearly cannot meet all the needs of 80 million Americans aged seventy or older. Yet we know that the vast majority of elder Americans—nearly 90 percent[1]—want to stay in their homes as long as possible. The people we rely on to make this possible are professional caregivers, those doing what Dr. Audrey Chun, the director of the renowned geriatric clinic at Mount Sinai Medical Center, calls "the job of ultimate importance in the health and quality of life of our parents."[2] This is the job of professional caregivers like Marlene Champion.

"A lot of people look down their noses at us," Marlene re-marks. "They don't think of it as real work: they think of house-work differently. Even some of your friends and family. One time when I was at a job, someone said to me, 'You call that working?'"

Marlene Champion was seventeen years old when she took her first job as a domestic worker, looking after three children of a well-off household in St. Michael, Barbados, where she was born and raised. "It was hard," she admits, "because I was still a child myself, and here I had to wash other people's clothes and cook their meals and mind their children. It was hard because I didn't really have a parent I could talk to or learn from."

She made $25 to $30 per week, which she used to support her-self and her first child. When she was thirty years old, Marlene took the savings she had tucked away over the years and came to the United States. She intended to stay for five years, send home some money and save some, and then return to her own children.

Her start in the United States was rough: months without work, spending down her tiny bit of savings. Finally a family friend—a friend of her sister's from Barbados employed as a domestic worker in New York—connected Marlene with a family who needed someone to look after their father, a retired pediatrician who was recovering from hip surgery. His name was Dr. Mor-ris Steiner. For some time his caregiver had been a woman from Belgium who spoke no English and spoon-fed him, bringing his meals on a tray. Bedridden, staring out the window or watching TV, Steiner was languishing, not recovering.

"On my first day, the family told me what was going on, and I asked him, 'Can you walk?' When he said yes, I told him that from that day on he would have his meals in the dining room.

The previous aide used to bring him everything on a tray and have him sitting and eating as if he couldn't feed himself. When you do that, you're keeping people in the position that they're not able to do it themselves. I fixed some lunch and put it on the table, and from then I had him coming to the table. Dr. Steiner's son and daughter-in-law looked at each other, like they decided about me in that moment: 'Okay, she is the one.'

"Then I started to work with him to bring him back. The house had three floors and he had been staying on the second floor. He wouldn't come downstairs because he had hip problems. He had had hip surgery and had been in a lot of pain. I coaxed him and coaxed him and coaxed him until I got him downstairs. I asked him to show me the office where he used to work.

"Then I tried to get him to come outside with me but he didn't want to go. He was scared. He had been watching TV and seen all the violence on the news. After months of coaxing him, I got him to step right outside the door. Then I had to coax him again until I could get him to the veranda. He would say to me, 'In two minutes, let's go back in.' I got him to sit out there. Then I'd get as far as pushing him around the block in the wheelchair. He started going to weddings and bar mitzvahs and other family gatherings when I escorted him. He had been homebound for six or seven years until then."

Much of Marlene's extraordinary skill as a caregiver lies in how she communicates. "Do you need help?" is how she approaches situations, giving people the option to help themselves first, to do things on their own terms. "Don't take away my independence," Steiner always said to her, and Marlene was happy to hear him say so. Often, Marlene notes, people speak to older adults and adults with disabilities—and children—as though doubting their capacity. Marlene treats everyone, regardless of age or ability, as if they are whole, equal, and unique. Her style of connecting quickly builds trust. "After a while, it was like I was a part of him and he was a part of me. Sometimes I would be sitting there around ten o'clock or so and I would get up and go make a cup of tea and bring it back to him. He would ask, 'How did you know I wanted that?' And I would say, 'I just know.' And he would say, 'Mental telepathy.' "

Marlene was a particularly good fit with Dr. Steiner and his family. Caregiving relationships can be challenging. Elders, like all of us, can be uncooperative, demanding, or moody. Their frustration and sadness about aging and death, as well as their fears about being ill or dependent on others, sometimes understandably get expressed as anger, irritability, or anxiety. Marlene notes, "You might have someone with dementia. Some of them lie—accusing you of things to their families. Some families believe them and think the worst of us; some don't. It takes a lot of patience. The person that you're caring for and the family both have a part in it, because if you are treated with respect, there's nothing that you wouldn't do or try to do to make that person comfortable. It's a two-way street."

Marlene was with Dr. Steiner until the end: "He didn't want to die with anybody else around but me. He didn't want to be in that place with nobody else. We had gotten so close and he loved me. I put my whole self into it. I took care of that man with my life."

After Dr. Steiner's death, Marlene started providing child care in upper Manhattan and met other nannies who were involved in Domestic Workers United, the New York organization of domestic workers I helped to start in 2000, a founding group in the National Domestic Workers Alliance. She became instrumental in our campaigns to win rights for domestic workers. In 2011, more than twenty-five years after arriving in the United States, she had finally saved enough money and was able to visit her family in Barbados, where her four sons, nine grandkids, and one great-granddaughter live.

Nicie Hassell was born in the Dominican Republic. Like Marlene, she began providing care in her home country, but Nicie got started even earlier. She was just eight years old when she became the primary caregiver for her newborn cousin. She had to wake at five each morning to feed him, watching her mother set off to work as a caregiver for other families. Nicie decided she wanted to be a nurse when she grew up.

Later Nicie had two daughters, who she raised as a single mother: Gabrielle and Stephanie, who are now eighteen and fourteen, respectively. She saved her money and sent them to the United States, where she felt they would have a better chance at success, joining them shortly afterward, once she could afford it, in 2011.

"Gabrielle wants to become a fashion designer. She has her own sewing machine. She creates her own designs," says Nicie, her face glowing with pride.

Nicie and her daughters share a house in New Jersey, although she is able to spend only a few days each month with them. She works as an in-home attendant for an elderly woman named Dolores who lives on Staten Island in New York City. Dolores has had Alzheimer's disease and dementia for more than a decade. She requires the help of four caregivers in order to remain in her own home, so Nicie shares the work with Ana, Theresa, and Wilma.

"The only thing Dolores can do on her own is eat," Nicie explains. "You have to remind her to do everything, like brush her teeth. But she doesn't like being reminded that she forgot something or that she has Alzheimer's." Nicie's duties include bathing Dolores and caring for her skin, which is prone to sores. She also pays bills, manages correspondence, and accompanies Dolores to her medical appointments.

Dolores is a lively talker. Every afternoon at four p.m. the women watch *Dr. Oz* together, and Dolores takes notes on every episode. They also watch romantic comedies, Dolores's favorite genre. The four caregivers take turns planning adventures for Dolores, such as trips to the local shopping center. They keep her laughing. Under the care of the four women, Dolores is thriving. She has gained thirty pounds, which the doctors say is unprecedented. There is no question Dolores is happier than she would be in an institutional setting.

Yet Dolores's well-being comes at the cost of Nicie's family's well-being, as is often the case with the children of women who work as professional caregivers. Nicie says she is raising her daughters via text messages. Still, she keeps in daily contact with them, giving her older daughter Gabrielle a wake-up call each morning at five. Stephanie, her younger daughter, calls her mom every day as she walks to school. "That way she feels safe," says Nicie.

Gabrielle is on medication for ADHD. Sometimes it makes her nauseous. "She only calls if she's having a bad day," says Nicie. "When I don't hear from her I know she's feeling okay." Nicie wishes she could be home cooking for her girls and supporting them, but the older they get, the more expenses there are, and Nicie doesn't want them to have to work yet. She insists on providing for them. She gives each girl an allowance every two weeks. The girls are her life, and she doesn't mind giving up her own interests to provide for them.

Once she even had to bring Dolores to their home in New Jersey. It was October 2012, and Hurricane Sandy, the deadliest and most destructive hurricane of that season, struck the New York area. The four caregivers grew anxious as the storm approached since Dolores's home is near the water, and they contacted Dolores's family in California to ask permission to bring Dolores somewhere safer. At first they went to Wilma's house, but when the power went out there, they moved Dolores to Nicie's home in New Jersey, where she would stay for two weeks. While the two teenagers were happy to have their mom cooking meals in their own kitchen for a change, it blurred already tenuous boundaries between home and work—Nicie literally had to bring her work home with her.

Nicie's daughters worry that Nicie never does anything for herself, but she points out that she has her special Saturdays to look forward to. On an occasional Saturday when she doesn't have to care for Dolores, Nicie takes the girls to the movies. "We arrive for the two p.m. matinee and we stay until eleven at night, seeing one after the other." She smiles indulgently.

Plus, Nicie still holds on to her dream of one day becoming a full-fledged nurse: maybe once her daughters are independent she will be able to pursue the degree that will legitimize all the years of actual nursing experience she has already acquired.

"If you give, you'll always get. When I help people, God always provides for me," says Nicie.

• • •

"Sometimes we need to be a psychologist, because we need to really understand why our client is like this so we can cope. Sometimes you have to be a singer because that is the only way your client will be calmed."

In a well-off suburb of Chicago, at the assisted living facility where she works, Erlinda sings mostly prayer songs and occasionally makes up her own lyrics to go with the melodies. She's discovered that singing is the simplest way to gain her clients' trust, which she describes as her number one goal. Erlinda believes singing is a universal form of communication, bridging cultures and generations.

Erlinda came to this country from the Philippines five years ago and has been working as a private caregiver in the Midwest since she arrived.

"I'm proud to say I come from the Philippines. There we take care of older people in our families, so it's in your heart already to take care of people who need help, and here in America we are paid to do that as our work."

Her children are in college and still living in the Philippines, with the exception of a daughter who lives in Singapore and works as a nurse. Every week without fail, Erlinda sends money home to her children and extended family. They count on her income to pay for food, housing, health care, and education. She hasn't seen her family back home for five years now. She believes that while working so far from her family is a tremendous sacrifice, ultimately it is worth it because she is able to help them economically.

Erlinda is in her early fifties, but her lively presence, her sporty short haircut, and the bright coral-colored jersey she was wearing when we met in the office of the Chicago Household Workers Association make her seem younger than her age. She takes noticeable care of her appearance; every hair sits perfectly in place, and her silver eye shadow accentuates her round eyes and matches the gauzy gray scarf draped around her neck. Erlinda believes strongly that personal hygiene and self-care must be a top priority for caregivers. "If we want to be seen as professionals, we have to be professional in every way, including looking presentable," she says. She also believes it's vital to stay healthy both physically and spiritually. "I pray—I just say, 'Lord, thank you for this day. I hope this day will come smoothly.' Praising God, I wake up and ask for his help that I will be able to deal with this day without problems. You have to start the day with positive thinking. Because it's not an easy job. You have to be physically, emotionally prepared.

"A recent client, Maria, came home from the hospital paralyzed on one side of her body. Things she took for granted her whole life, she could not do, including the most basic things like talking. It was so hard for her to accept this, and the family also could not accept it. They did not know that she was emotionally devastated. She could not speak. Only I knew, because she was moody, and she would physically fight me to stop me from touching her. The stroke left her right body paralyzed, so her speech was affected but her brain was working. So she could understand what was going on but she needed assistance, including for walking.

"She was incontinent, too, so I had to check on her all through the night. Every minute, every day and night you think about her—*How is she? Is she wet?* There are also times she can have accidents in the bed. You have to take her out, bring her to the shower, and clean her up at two in the morning. There is no set time. It's 'as needed.' You cannot say, 'I'll deal with it tomorrow.' You just have to do it.

"There is no day or night for a caregiver. We are the first to wake. The day starts at five or six o'clock in the morning. We are also the last ones to go to sleep. In the Philippines we call it *tulug manok*. You know how the chicken sleeps? It is already part of your brain, or already a habit to wake when the first light of day appears at your bedroom window. Your body knows, *Oh, it's time to get up.*

"We do all this and yet can I say we are the most unappreciated workers on this planet? People think that we are just doing the dirty jobs, cleaning the toilets. When you are a caregiver, you do clean the toilet, but you also cook, give them their medicines, talk to them, entertain them, heal them. You do what is needed to support your client in what they need. It requires someone to understand their needs on every level, and how to handle so many situations.

"Some people say, 'You just wipe ass,' which is really humiliating. Or they say to me, 'You are just a caregiver.' As if you are down, down below them. We are not *just* caregivers; we are one of the most important members of a household. Caregiving is not a humiliating job; it's like a teacher or doctor or any other profession. It's not easy, and it has dignity."

Before coming to Chicago, Erlinda worked as a caregiver in Wisconsin. She worked for a home care agency that specifically recruited newly arrived immigrant women without family in the United States because they were vulnerable. They were required to live at the agency and be on call. She was asked to keep a small overnight bag packed at all times, in case she was called out to work. They were paid less than minimum wage for live-in work, often in challenging environments, including caring for people with Alzheimer's.

Erlinda remembers one client in particular. She had just arrived in the country and had very little experience. The man she was caring for was a retired actor with Alzheimer's. With the support of caregivers, he and his wife lived at home. His wife was in good health, was much younger than he was, and took her frustration out on Erlinda, often yelling insults at Erlinda and calling her stupid. The man regularly asked Erlinda to trim his pubic hair and frequently offered her extra money to masturbate him. Erlinda refused his requests but lived in fear of the repercussions for her employment and immigration status. To this day she is hesitant to work with men, particularly those who live alone.

While working at the same agency, she also worked with Jake and Dorothy, a couple who deeply valued her support. Jake was recovering from surgery at home and Erlinda worked the second shift, the night shift, relieving another caregiver. Jake couldn't walk after his surgery, but over many weeks of patient encouragement, Erlinda helped him walk again.

"They were good people; they let me sleep when they didn't need me."

The more time that went by, the more Jake and Dorothy wanted Erlinda to stay on a more permanent basis, and the more they wanted to put her onto a payroll system. One day they asked for her Social Security number, and because she was undocumented and afraid of being reported, she immediately left the job. She made up a story about having to return to the Philippines. Today she deeply regrets that decision.

"I was proud of the work I did there. I wish I had told the truth. They might have been able to help me. When you support people and build trust, you can make miracles happen."

Every Sunday, Erlinda goes to church and prays. After a difficult week, she releases all of her emotions while kneeling in the pew. "You just have to look around to make sure that no one sees that you are crying. And you pray that the Lord can give you the strength to manage all of these things."

Erlinda insists that there are many good experiences of caregiving in this country. Another tender memory Erlinda shares with me is of a ninety-two-year-old client whom Erlinda called "my lady," who loved to have Erlinda sing to her.

"My lady always said, 'Give me your hand,' so I sat by her bedside, took her hand, and sang to her. One day I could see from her face that she was leaving us. She looked peaceful, like she was ready. I was proud that I could be there for that transition, to be with her in that moment." Together with the family, Erlinda witnessed the passing of her beloved "lady."

At the wake, Erlinda was asked by the son to stand. In front of the family and friends who had gathered, he explained who Erlinda was and thanked her for the care and support she had provided his mother. The family asked her to stay and work as a housekeeper, but she told them, "Perhaps another older person like your mother needs me more," and moved on.

Marlene, Nicie, and Erlinda are three of the estimated 2 million people—mostly women—who work as in-home caregivers in the United States, enabling the people they support to lead full and dignified lives despite illness, frailty, or disability. While they often serve as nutritionists, teachers, physical therapists, psycho-therapists, emergency responders, drivers, personal organizers, and nurses, the most precious services they provide are often physical and emotional: compassion, tenderness, and listening. They provide company for those whose working days are done and who deserve their portion of ease and comfort in their older years. They reignite our pride in the accomplishments of our lives. They listen; they get to know our family's quirks, vulnerabilities, and secrets. They hold our hands, sing for us, comb our hair.

Caregivers are also the workers who are most consistently in contact with the most costly clients of our health care system. They substantially cut health care costs by helping to manage chronic illnesses and by supporting people so that they can stay in their homes and out of radically more expensive institutions. During and immediately following natural disasters or other catastrophes, caregivers are the unsung heroes, usually responding before the first responders by choosing to stay with their clients to see them through to safety—even when it means not going home to look after their own families.

Their work goes beyond their relationship with their client as well. As the previous chapter explains, family members of elders frequently experience their own anxieties and fear of loss, alongside frustration and guilt that they cannot provide the care themselves. They may feel shame, as if they've failed in their familial obligations; they may become hopeless or depressed. The tensions between siblings may become explosive. A professional caregiver entering the situation can help alleviate these feelings. She often serves as a sort of mediator or counselor amid fraught family relations. In this way, care work supports not only the elder or person with disabilities, but the functioning of the entire family as well.

Undeniably, the work is rooted in relationships and emotions. One way of understanding this is that the basic values that define all healthy relationships between people—respect, humanity, accountability, dignity, empathy, and compassion—also apply here. Nothing about the relational aspects of caregiving makes it any less of a real job. Caregiving is most definitely work: physically strenuous, rigorous work that requires discernment and flexibility. As with all forms of labor, you put in a hard day's work and you expect to be appreciated and compensated. You strive to do better and learn more, and you expect to advance over the course of a full career. You take pride in your work and expect to be able to support your family.

The Care Labyrinth

Caregivers work in a variety of settings, under a variety of titles, and are paid for in a variety of ways—all of which adds to the challenge of acknowledging the value of their work, of bringing workers together, and of improving their working conditions.

The overarching technical terms for those whose job is to support someone's health and human service needs are "direct service workers," "direct care workers," or "direct support professionals." These people who work with elders and individuals with disabilities fall into one of three categories according to the Bureau of Labor Statistics: "certified nursing assistant" (the direct care workers in nursing homes, "home health aide" (workers who provide in-home skilled nursing care after a hospital or facility stay), and "personal care assistant" (the formal occupational title for home care workers). Of these, the first two jobs are usually licensed, regulated occupations that involve medical responsibilities and training outside the scope of a personal care assistant.

Personal care assistants, in turn, are often also referred to as "personal assistants," "personal care attendants," "home care aides," "individual or independent providers," "home care providers," and "home attendants." Often "housekeepers," "cleaners," and other domestic workers like nannies do the work of personal care assistants—often informally and without appropriate compensation or recognition. When I refer to "caregivers" and "care workers," I am talking about all those personal care assistants and domestic workers who provide the primarily nonmedical home care services I described in the previous sections.

Employers of paid caregivers are either individuals or agencies, which can be either for-profit or private, nonprofit companies. Agencies may have a contract with the state to serve Medicaid clients, or may solicit clients who pay privately—or both. Co-op models are also emerging, in which workers themselves create a registry of available care providers and negotiate the conditions of employment.

For most middle-income people, the elder herself—or a family member—becomes the employer. The potential employer typically asks around in the community or looks in the classified section of the local paper to find a caregiver, sometimes known as a "gray market aide." The caregiver may or may not have received formal training and may or may not have legal immigration status. Some have worked as health care professionals, such as nurses, in their countries of origin. As the employer, the family or the individual pays the worker and is responsible for employment taxes and deductions and appropriate insurance coverage such as workers' compensation, in case the caregiver is injured while providing care in the home. Not every employer is aware of these requirements or willing to provide them.

Often these individual employment arrangements involve no written contracts, and neither the employer/client nor the worker has clarity around hours, safety standards, responsibilities, and rights. In fact, many individual employers don't consider themselves formal employers at all—they just think of themselves as paying for "a little help."

With an agency as employer, the rate charged to clients is higher, as the agency handles contracts, taxes and deductions, workers' compensation, general liability, and bonding insurance—and takes a profit. Unfortunately, the higher cost does not always translate into higher wages for caregivers or better care for the client. Agencies also can offer substitute caregivers if the primary one gets sick. In general, the client cannot choose her or his caregiver in this model but is assigned one by the agency. Agencies sometimes provide training and certification in skills such as CPR and first aid.

Caregivers employed by agencies are more likely to have employer-provided health insurance—approximately one in four do, compared with fewer than one in five workers employed by private employers. Pension plans are even less frequently provided: one in ten privately employed care workers participates in an employer pension plan.[3] Paid vacation and sick leave are rare, regardless of employment status.

In certain states, the government serves as the formal employer of record for independent providers who support Medicaid clients. In California, for example, the In-Home Supportive Services program functions in tandem with a consumer-directed model: the client or his or her family hires and fires the caregiver, and the consumer or family "directs" or supervises the plan of care for which the state has authorized payment. Timesheets are submitted to the county and then forwarded to the state of California, which pays workers as though they were selling services to the state. Other states, on the basis of local policy or state rules on funding streams, have a mix of employment structures, including both individual employers and agencies.

Agency-employed caregivers can't administer medications for state regulation or liability reasons and are usually not permitted to use their client's credit card or car, which complicates common tasks such as shopping or doctors' appointments.

More than 40 percent of all direct care providers work less than full-time. Those employed by agencies are more likely to have placements or assignments to multiple clients that make up full-time employment, but those hired by individuals must juggle the needs and often erratic schedules of their clients, not to mention transportation between work sites, if they want to cobble together part-time jobs to reach full-time employment. Having multiple clients does enable a caregiver to diversify her income streams and to compare the standards in various situations, alleviating, at least a little, the isolation that characterizes these jobs.

Isolation, and its positive twin, autonomy, are defining characteristics of the work. Working inside a home means there is no break room or water cooler where workers can compare stories or get input on challenges from their peers. Even workers employed by agencies don't develop relationships with other workers or staff at the agency, often receiving only notifications of schedule changes and no further contact. If a client mistreats or accuses a caregiver of misconduct, there is no one around to witness what happened. The flipside is autonomy, which many care workers value about their chosen profession: no nasty office dynamics to contend with, no manager looking over one's shoulder, and the freedom to arrange one's tasks and the flow of the day.

The isolation also creates a huge challenge in improving the situation of workers. Unlike most workplaces, where the number of employees exceeds the number of employers, and there's the potential for collective negotiation and action, there is generally only one domestic worker in a home. This relationship puts the caregiver in a vulnerable position. When you add a difference in class between employer and caregiver to the equation, and especially if the care worker is an undocumented immigrant, her situation becomes even more vulnerable. It was this reality that led to the creation of Domestic Workers United in New York in 2000, and in 2007, the National Domestic Workers Alliance. Domestic workers include elder caregivers, but the organization brings together everyone who works in private homes, including housekeepers, nannies, caregivers for elders, and attendants for people with disabilities.

Domestic workers have always been treated as a "special class" of workers; they have been "specially" undervalued as workers and excluded from labor laws since the New Deal. This special treatment is rooted in the legacy of slavery. Farmwork and domestic work had been the work of slaves, so when labor laws were passed in the 1930s, southern members of Congress refused to sign on to the labor law package as part of the New

Deal if farmworkers and domestic workers—who at the time were largely African Americans—were included. In the deal that Congress struck, those two workforces were excluded.

A significant step forward was made in 2013, when, as a result of our and many others organizations' efforts, the U.S. Department of Labor released a regulatory change that narrows the exclusion of "companions" from the Fair Labor Standards Act, so that nearly 2 million home care providers and caregivers will be covered under minimum wage and overtime protections starting January 1, 2015. After seventy-five years of exclusion, we're finally beginning to recognize and establish basic protections for care work.

But we can do more to take advantage of the tremendous economic opportunity represented by professional caregiving. Home care workers are the fastest growing workforce in the country. The current situation of the eldercare workforce—low wages, long hours, inadequate training, and little chance for career advancement—has led to high turnover in the industry and a resultant low quality of care for people who need it.

Erlinda mentioned how caregiving work is really no different from the work of teachers or doctors. I draw hope from the fact that all sorts of professions, especially those considered "women's jobs," were valued much less than they are today or even derided: teachers, for sure; nurses, too. Yet slowly they have become more professionalized, respected, understood, and valued. Caregiving is on the cusp of that discovery now.

Yet as it stands now, the people America's families are counting on to meet our most fundamental needs are not being well cared for in return.

Unrequited Care

Professional caregivers work inside our homes; the site of our most intimate experiences is their workplace. They spend weeks, months, and often years in this private sphere, taking care of our most personal physical and emotional needs. Nothing is hidden from them. Yet the intimate nature of the work can become a real challenge when caregivers negotiate for fair compensation. The situation is particularly confusing for employers, who are sometimes haunted by the question: if it's done for money, is the affection authentic? *If you really love my family, won't you do anything for us?* For the worker, being treated as "part of the family" ideally translates to respect, bonuses, and benefits. For the employer, "being part of the family" too often means extra favors and no boundaries—the caregiver is required to be available all the time. With tragic frequency, workers feel heartbroken or frustrated that employers—and society at large—don't automatically recognize the tremendous value of their work.

Instead, too often, "I think that some people still think that slavery is okay," Marlene Champion says wearily. In return for the wide-ranging life-sustaining services that care workers provide, they earn, on average, less than $10 per hour. Few receive paid vacation or sick days, despite the high rate of injury and burnout associated with care work. Most workers are subject to termination without notice and without severance pay.

In 2012, the University of Illinois at Chicago and the National Domestic Workers Alliance released *Home Economics*, the first-ever national survey of domestic workers—nannies and housekeepers as well as caregivers. With responses from more than two thousand women in fourteen cities across the United States, the study found that nearly one-quarter of domestic workers receive pay beneath the minimum wage, that they rarely receive employment benefits, and that many experience abuse and disrespect on the job. More than 90 percent of those who encounter problems with their working conditions do not raise the issue with their employer because they are afraid of being fired. In fact, nearly a quarter of the domestic workers surveyed had been fired from a job after they complained about unsafe working conditions. Respondents also described many cases of wage theft, when workers were paid less than was agreed upon or not paid at all.[4]

I was not surprised by these findings because they are in line with what I hear every day. The hundreds of stories I've heard—and other anecdotal evidence from the field—indicate that professional caregivers face high rates of depression from isolation, separation from their own families, stress, and fatigue. Their work is often difficult and unstable. As a result, rates of burnout and turnover are alarmingly high. Although comprehensive nationwide data do not exist, the stories I hear mirror what a 2007 report found after analyzing a variety of state-based studies:

> The AHCA survey of nursing homes found annual turnover rates among nurse aides of more than 76 percent and vacancy rates of almost 12 percent. . . . A 2005 American Association of Retired Persons (AARP) report cites numerous studies of high vacancy and turnover rates among paraprofessional direct care staff. . . . One national study of assisted living reported annual turnover rates of about 40 percent among personal care workers and nurse aides. A 2002 Wisconsin study found turnover rates among direct

care paraprofessionals of 77 percent to 164 percent in assisted living, from 99 percent to 127 percent in nursing homes and 25 percent to 50 percent in home health agencies. A 2002 North Carolina study found turnover rates for aides of 95 percent in nursing homes and 37 percent for home care agencies.

Depending on the study, as many as one-quarter of workers who left a home care job did not take another job in home care work but left the field. Workers cited dissatisfaction with their pay, hours of work, and benefits, heavy workloads, and lack of support as reasons for quitting.[5]

I think of Diki, a caregiver from Nepal. Diki worked as a live-in for an employer who often woke her at two a.m. to demand a cup of tea; who gave Diki just a mat on the living room floor for her sleeping quarters; and who, as the ultimate bargaining chip, held on to Diki's passport. An immigrant worker without legal status, Diki had little in the way of rights or recourse and few prospects for improving her situation. If only Diki's story were rare or exceptional. It is not.

Indispensable Immigrants

Immigration issues are inseparable from the issue of caregiving. According to *Home Economics*, two-thirds of nannies, housekeepers, and caregivers for the elderly are foreign-born, and about half of them are undocumented. The study also found that 85 percent of undocumented domestic workers working in substandard conditions do not complain because they fear their immigration status will be used against them.[6]

Foreign-born women coming to the United States to provide caregiving are part of a larger pattern of international labor migration. Because farming no longer provides a sustainable livelihood in parts of the globe where it was once the primary means of survival, people there are forced to leave and find work in industrialized nations. As the world has become more globalized, cities like New York and Los Angeles have become home to the corporate professionals who are busy overseeing global industries. These professionals have needs that are met by service workers who work at the other end of the wage spectrum, including taxi drivers, delivery people, security guards, and domestic workers. And then there are the low-wage workers who service the service workers: small businesses in working-class neighborhoods that meet the needs of domestic workers and others.

Recent immigrants end up in these urban centers because there is such a large demand for their labor there. This demographic reality has been steadily spreading from large urban centers to more and more municipalities, states, and even rural areas, places that are less dense, fast growing, and entrepreneurial. Today it's difficult to imagine how the country would function without immigrants. Immigrants grow, harvest, and package our food; they drive us to the airport, pump our gas, and serve and clear away our food in restaurants. They take care of the most precious elements of our lives—our homes and families.

According to the calculations of Dowell Myers, professor of demography and coauthor with Stephen Levy and John Pitkin of *Immigrants and Boomers*, between replacing retired workers and new workforce growth in the coming decades, we'll need more than 82 million people entering the workforce. Thirty-five to 40 percent of that workforce will have to come from first- and second-generation immigrants.[7] Overall the immigrant population is younger than the general U.S. population, thanks to young migrants (aged twenty-five to forty-four) who have arrived in the United States since the 1980s and to higher birth rates among immigrants than in the general population.

In fact, we are counting on immigrants not only to fill jobs as the baby boomers retire but also to buy houses, to buy other goods and services, to accumulate wealth, and to pay taxes. Dowell Myers believes that "failure to examine how much immigrants typically advance over time leads to the false conclusion that they are trapped in poverty and impose an economic burden on society. . . . Immigrant homebuyers are crucial in buying homes from the increasing number of older Americans. Immigrants will clearly be important in leading us out of the current housing downturn." His research found that 64 percent of Latino immigrants who have lived in California for more than ten years own their own homes.[8]

Despite our increasing reliance on them, many immigrants are forced to navigate work while living in fear of separation from their own families as a result of immigration status. Many remain excluded and in the shadows. Not only do the undocumented live in fear of deportation, they have challenges with every aspect of life—signing a lease, opening a bank account, receiving health care, traveling, working; nothing is simple when you're undocumented. Immigrants are the invisible infrastructure of this economy and our social fabric. They are everywhere, and nowhere are they secure.

Since 2009, the United States has deported nearly 2 million undocumented immigrants. Many of them have been in the United States for ten or even twenty years, so long that they have no one to call when they land back in their home country. Women are often told that they have to sign off on voluntary deportation papers or agree to be guilty of criminal charges, with the carrot that they'll be able to be reunited with their children. Once you self-deport, though, you can't come back. It's resulting in women being separated from their children without the hope of ever coming back.

I witnessed a brave young woman named Eliza testify before Congress on the impact of being separated from her mother, who was deported:

Dear Members of Congress,

My name is Eliza Morales. I am 19 years old, and I was born in Los Angeles. I want you to hear my story, and I want this story to help you understand why immigration laws need to change now. In 2008, when I was fourteen, my mother was stopped at an immigration checkpoint while she was driving to pick me up at school. While I waited, and she didn't come, I imagined she was working late or might've been caught in traffic due to a rainy afternoon. I finally went home and waited and worried. Two days passed by with no sign of her and then I finally got a call from my mother. She was in Tijuana, and she told me she had gotten deported. There is no feeling that can compare to what I felt that night besides death. I felt totally empty and alone.

I imagined that my mom would only be away for a while, so for the time being I moved to my godmother's house in a small town called Union City in California. For a whole year I didn't make many friends in the belief that I would soon go back to Los Angeles where I'm from and start from where I left off. But one year passed by and I realized that there was no hope of my mom returning to the United States. I started to feel and think that maybe she had abandoned me.

I started my sophomore year in high school in Union City, and made friends even though they weren't leading me in the right direction. I started to think school wasn't worth going to. I would have to say that my sophomore year was one of the most life changing years for me because I didn't have my mom with me, and during that year I moved 3 times. The first time I moved was because my godmother lost her house and it was hard to be financially stable. The second time I moved was because I started getting out of hand. I had bad grades, skipped school, and hung out with the wrong crowd. I was forced to live with an aunt. During that time I felt hopeless, empty, and displaced. None of this would have happened if my mother was here. My teenage years were when I needed her the most, but she had been taken away from me.

Finally, I decided that I wanted to move back to LA. I was angry at the fact that I couldn't be happy away from her. I was embarrassed at the fact that I was living in a white community and within that community I felt I was the only one who didn't have her parents' guidance. I was keeping all my emotions bottled up and kept them to myself. There was a point where I couldn't take it anymore. But I decided that I needed to take action and try to take control of my life.

So I moved back to LA and moved in with an aunt. I started going to school every day and found myself a job. I started to realize that it wasn't my mother's fault nor mine, but it was the policies that were separating us and keeping us from being happy! At that time I felt I was being betrayed by my own country. All the moving I had gone through made my mother lose track of where I was and it wasn't easy keeping contact with her so I scheduled a weekend to visit her. I went down to Tijuana to see her, and during that visit, I met many people interested in the injustice my mother and I had gone through. So I became involved to make a difference. That's why I am here today. And that's why I am closer to my mother than ever before; because I've realized that our love is stronger than any border.

Eliza's testimony reveals the nature of the interaction between the U.S. immigration system and the child welfare system, which results in children being separated from their parents. In the fourteen months between July 1, 2010, and September 31, 2012, a total of 204,810 deportations were issued for parents with U.S. citizen children, according to federal data unearthed by the Applied Research Center. Researchers conservatively calculate that about 1.25 percent of the children in foster care in the United States are in this situation and that at this rate, at least fifteen thousand more children will face separation from their detained and deported parents in the next five years.

Although both immigration laws and child welfare policies state their explicit aims to keep families united,[9] in practice, citizen children are often moved into foster care when their immigrant parents are detained or deported. For example, to regain custody and bring their children to Mexico with them, Mexican American parents must go through an arduous bureaucratic process of proving themselves to be fit and capable, a process that can take a year or more. Held in an immigrant detention center hundreds of miles away from the courthouse, parents are often unable to attend the dependency court hearings because their court-appointed attorneys cannot locate and notify them or because their wardens at U.S. Immigration and Customs Enforcement refuse to transport them to the court. From the perspective of Child Protective Services, this is the parents' fault, and it too often results in the termination of parental rights; the child is then put up for adoption.

I've also heard stories about parents winning their claim and managing to bring their children to Mexico. But the kids couldn't assimilate: they didn't speak Spanish or know the culture; they didn't have friends; the Mexican school system is different. Mexico is not home for them. Some parents try to send the kids back to the United States with "coyotes," or traffickers. The process is excruciating, yet people do it for a better life for their families.

Among the domestic workers I know, almost all of them came to the United States because they wanted to create a better life for their children and because they wanted to support their families back home. How doubly cruel, having experienced the indignities and sacrifices that go along with being an undervalued worker, to then be ripped apart from new families here in the United States—both the ones for whom they provide care and their own children born in the United States. No one responsible for caring for the most precious elements of our lives—our homes and our families—should be at risk of being torn from their homes and families as a result of the United States' immigration policies.

The truth is, the diverse and growing aging population and the growing immigrant population in this country need each other. We have three times more families in need of care providers than our current workforce is able to support. There is no way to meet our need for care in this country without immigrants carrying a lot of the weight.

Women's Work

As well as being associated with the unpaid work of slaves, and then the poorly paid work of African Americans and immigrants, caregiving is and has always been associated with women, alongside other kinds of unpaid work in the home: homemaking, childbearing, and child rearing. Providing love, care, and companionship are considered women's "natural" skills and therefore not monetizable. They simply have not been counted within our economy's measures of productivity. It has just been assumed that women will perform them. And women have done it—whether as unpaid and underacknowledged family caregivers or as low-paid professional caregivers, home care workers, and domestic workers.

An influential article by Gloria Steinem called "Revaluing Economics" names the two fundamental resources that underlie everything else in the economy and society: the planet's natural resources and the energy that goes into raising families. These are the two major resources that have been made invisible in our current socioeconomic system. Not only are those resources invisible; their exploitation is assumed. We have assumed that women will care for families, whether or not they work outside the home as well, as much as we have assumed that there will always be more freshwater to drink and cheap gas to pump.

"Take the economic vacuum called 'women who don't work,' " writes Steinem. "Almost every woman knows this economic invisibility in some part of her life. Whether or not she is in the paid labor force, a major part of her energy is probably devoted to productive work within the family and household, work that isn't counted as work at all." [10] Writing in the early 1990s, Steinem calculated that the gross national product of the United States would rise by 26 percent if homemakers' labor were included, while Statistics Canada, that country's information-gathering agency, estimated a single year of homemakers' work at $200 billion, or almost 40 percent of Canada's GDP.

More recently, sociologist Arlie Hochschild and economist Nancy Folbre have researched the dynamics of care work. In a 2012 interview, Folbre said, "The common notion that we inhabit two disparate worlds—one in which we do things for love, and one in which we do things for money—has some very perverse effects. It justifies a distinct lack of respect and remuneration for work that involves love and also justifies the pursuit of naked self-interest where money is concerned. It's a very gendered distinction—women are to love as men are to money." [11] Hochschild writes:

> The value of the labour of raising a child—always low relative to the value of other kinds of labour—has, under the impact of globalization, sunk lower still. Children matter to their parents immeasurably, of course, but the labour of raising them does not earn much credit in the eyes of the world. When middle-class housewives raised children as an unpaid, full-time role, the work was dignified by its

aura of middle-classness. That was the one upside to the otherwise confining cult of middle-class, nineteenth- and early-twentieth-century American womanhood. But when the unpaid work of raising a child became the paid work of child-care workers, its low market value revealed the abidingly low value of caring work generally—and further lowered it.

The low value placed on caring work results neither from an absence of a need for it nor from the simplicity or ease of doing it. Rather, the declining value of childcare results from a cultural politics of inequality.[12]

Women have learned through a lifetime of material experiences and cultural cues, in subtle and not so subtle ways, that they must work twice as hard for less pay. Even now women are still overrepresented in positions of vulnerability and underrepresented in positions of power and influence. Despite the fact that women achieve higher levels of education—in 2011 women received 57 percent of bachelor's degrees, 60 percent of master's degrees, and 52 percent of doctoral degrees[13]—only 23 percent of university presidents, 26 percent of professors,[14] and fewer than than 5 percent of CEOs in Fortune's top 1000 companies are women.[15] In the 535 seats in the 113th U.S. Congress, women held 101: 20 in the Senate and 81 in the House. It's a record-breaking number, but still: less than 19 percent. The income gap persists such that women still earn an average of eighty cents for every dollar a man makes (women who pursue law earn nearly $1.5 million less than their male equivalents over the life of their careers![16])—and the *wealth* gap is much higher, with women owning only 36 percent as much wealth as men.[17] The statistics are even bleaker for women of color.

Women represent two-thirds of the minimum-wage workforce. Studies show that as occupations gain a higher percentage of female workers, the pay for those jobs goes down relative to wages in similar jobs that remain male dominated. Yet the main sectors of the economy that are growing have historically been associated with women, particularly service and health care work.

As more and more women enter the workforce, and as we live longer—causing more of us to need support to live independently—it becomes increasingly untenable for care work to go unrecognized, and more important, undervalued. Care work contributes significantly to the nation's productivity, yet its historical exclusion from measures of GDP further devalues professional paid care work. By acknowledging that homemakers' labor is a vital part of the U.S. economy, we begin to correct the assumption that care work is not real work.

As we hear in the sandwich generation stories, unpaid family caregivers are under tremendous invisible pressure, and that pressure is only increasing as more women work outside the home. Without a system to support caregiving, women and their families are stuck trying to figure out a way to get their family caregiving work done, and done well, in isolation—hiring an undocumented worker, trying to find a nanny in the neighborhood, or posting the position on Craigslist. It's something so important to us—who cares for our loved ones. Yet, as a nation, we have simply not taken the question seriously, mainly because we assume women will just do this work on top of everything else. Well, every day that mode of operating becomes less and less feasible.

In the coming era, the productive nature of care work can no longer be underestimated. The economy of the future needs to reevaluate our most fundamental resources, including life itself. It's simple and elegant: we need to respect and value the foundations on which everything else in our human society is built—relationships, nurturing, and home, as well as natural resources including clean water and air and healthy food. When we give credit where credit is due—at this deep level—everything else in society will suddenly stand on more sustainable, solid ground.

What happens to caregivers when they grow older and need care themselves?

At the end of her career providing care for others, sixty-six-year-old Diony Verdaguer is gradually retiring. This means working less, not entirely by choice. As she has aged, it has become harder to both find work and do the actual work. But she's still looking. She still needs to send money home to her family in the Philippines and to save for her own health care and retirement. Thankfully she received a spot in government-subsidized housing, a small one-bedroom apartment in a senior housing complex in Chicago; otherwise, she could not afford a roof over her head.

Travel has always been a passion of hers; this and the drive to support her family brought her to the United States in 2004 from Atimonan, Quezon, in the Philippines. Over the years, Diony has collected trinkets and ornaments like memories; they fill every corner of her small home. Many of these items have an Asian origin, like the series of three paintings of cherry blossoms hanging over the wall by the stove. Every time she hosts the Filipino American Grandparents Association meeting in her apartment, she is proud to share the meaning behind them. The Grandparents Association has an annual public celebration, and this year she's been diligently rehearsing a Broadway medley with the choral group. She's excited that the medley includes songs from her favorite musical, *The Sound of Music*.

After showing me the most significant items in her collection, Diony insists on feeding me. She ladles out a bowl of "macaroni soup." It has a light, milky broth with elbow macaroni and several kinds of meats, most of which I can't identify, with the exception of sausage. The eclectic mix mirrors the décor in her small apartment. She's a very good cook; all of her clients have wanted her to make Filipino food for them. She's introduced many Chicago seniors to chicken adobo, pansit, and other soft foods in the Philippine cuisine, which make swallowing easy.

Diony has often taken care of people with Alzheimer's, the most challenging clients of all. Her last clients were a couple, an eighty-eight-year-old woman with Alzheimer's and her ninety-two-year-old husband. "She didn't want to take a bath or stand up. I just took my time; I waited for her. Oh, it takes a lot of patience. I worked there a little less than five years. They had no more money, put her in the nursing home, then three months later she died. The husband just died last May. That's why I have no work."

Diony's own mother in the Philippines has Alzheimer's, and Diony pays for her caregiver. "I don't want her here in a nursing home, so I'm sending money. That's why I am looking for a new job. It's been more than five years since I worked through an agency, but I'm applying now."

She lives in fear of getting sick, being unable to work, and getting put in a nursing home here in the United States. "I don't want to go to a nursing home. They have a lot of patients; it's hard for them to attend to you. They don't take care of you there. A friend of my sister went to one and they didn't give her food. I'd rather go home to the Philippines. If we get sick, there are people to take care of us."

For now, Diony has bills to pay. She doesn't have a savings plan. She keeps on caring for others.

As we envision a future in which we take care of America's families across generations, we must create systems that adequately honor and compensate Diony, Marlene, Nicie, Erlinda, and the millions of other workers providing care. In a fair economy, the people whose profession is to raise children would not have trouble feeding or caring for their own children, and the people who provide care for our elders would receive support for their own retirement. In the caring future we must create, we will honor, respect, and value the precious labor that these workers provide: the care upholding our society.

The independence and productivity we treasure as individuals of all ages, and as a nation, require the work of caregivers at their foundation. With appropriate pay, benefits, and employee supports such as child care and transportation, alongside training and real career ladders, these can be respectable, family-sustaining jobs. Turning caregiving jobs into dignified jobs will have a ripple effect on society, on the economy, and on our spiritual health. By doing so, we affirm the dignity of people at every stage of life, into old age, and in every walk of life, including caregiving.

PART II

Care at the Crossroads

The United States is undergoing tremendous transformations. An unprecedented number of people are turning sixty-five, with those eighty-five and older becoming our fastest-growing age-group. Our demographics are shifting racially as well. Immigration has always been a huge force in shaping America, and it continues to be. The growing presence of women in every corner of the workforce is another enormous, yet not entirely visible or acknowledged, aspect of today's America that intersects with care. Additionally, across the globe, work itself is in flux. It is no longer so obvious what constitutes a workplace and how the economic and political system can support new kinds of work. Finally, yet another shift is under way in government, with increasing threats to our public social programs and "entitlements." So much about the way we live, work, and dream in the United States is shifting. Each of these trends impacts how we provide, compensate, and value care.

As these tremendous shifts happen in the United States, we are struggling with who we are going to become. The question is, how do we work together toward more prosperity, more humanity, more respect, and more dignity for everyone? On the one hand, our changing demographics could mean increasing polarization, particularly in light of our failing economy. We already see the anxieties of U.S. citizens being pitted against the interests of immigrants. Immigrants are blamed for the jobs crisis. Poor people, working mothers, and unions are blamed for the debt crisis.

Rather, as the environmental and civil rights leader Van Jones says, "This is a moment to turn to one another, not turn *on* one another."[1] I believe that in turning to one another, not only do we begin to heal the pain and trauma that has accumulated, but we also create better solutions. We learn about one another, see the problems more clearly, and develop more comprehensive and effective answers. Ultimately, we can't afford *not* to turn to one another.

Turning to one another means rendering visible how we are already, and have always been, interconnected through care. Nearly as invisible as the oxygen we breathe, and yet just as essential, care is the beating heart of our nation. Care is at the core of the conversation about and among America's elders and families. It's a conversation that intersects with issues of health care, government support programs, and the work of professional caregivers, such that talking about one of these issues unavoidably means including the others. Yet beyond that, I've come to see that what we talk about when we talk about care actually touches everyone, of every age and gender, doing every kind of work.

From the moment we're born, before we recognize our membership in any group, even before we identify our gender, we are dependent on the nurturing of another. We rely on our parents or whoever cares for us when we're young and can't care for ourselves. Even the most self-reliant adults are connected to a system that helps meet their basic needs. When we get sick, we once again need care. More often than not, we shift between being recipients of care and being providers of care. Care roots us in the interconnectedness of the world.

In my work, care has emerged as the connective tissue that can keep our diverse interests aligned. Despite our perceived differences, Americans are all in the same boat. When we keep our feet firmly rooted in this common ground, we can truly hear and see one another and find the solutions we need. This is the path of love. When you love someone, it's because you see through the differences that separate you from him or her, and you understand and feel the experience of interconnectedness. From there, we can work together respectfully across differences of opinion and experience to create a caring America.

"Every day when I arrive, I wake her up, I help her get dressed. Then we take deep breaths together before I prepare her breakfast," says Miriam Guillen, caregiver for Aminita Valles, with more than ten years of experience caring for elders. PHOTOGRAPH BY ALESSANDRA SANGUINETTI

4

WAKING THE
CARING MAJORITY

Love recognizes no barriers.
It jumps hurdles, leaps fences, penetrates walls
to arrive at its destination full of hope.
  —Maya Angelou,
    etched into the border wall near Tijuana

The concept of the Caring Majority came to me during a six-year legislative battle to establish basic rights for domestic workers in the state of New York.

In June 2009, I went on *The Brian Lehrer Show* on WNYC radio with Barbara Young, a longtime nanny in New York City, and Donna Schneiderman, a nanny employer in Brooklyn, to talk about the Domestic Workers' Bill of Rights legislation we had pending with the New York State legislature. Right before my segment, Lehrer spoke to New York's then governor David Paterson. He mentioned to the governor that we were in the studio and asked him about his position on the bill of rights. The governor replied, "The exclusion of domestic workers and farm-workers from labor rights is the legacy of a long history of racism. When this bill comes to my desk, I will sign it."

This was the first time anyone had heard the governor express support for the bill. We were all overwhelmed with emotion. When we were on live radio in the WNYC studio, Lehrer asked me why I was crying. My voice wavering, I answered that this was an amazing moment, after more than seventy years of exclusion from labor laws, and after our many years of campaigning, to hear that New York's governor was with us.

It felt like we were going to make history, and in fact, we did.

On August 31, 2010, I joined dozens of domestic workers at the historic, standing-room-only ceremony as the bill was signed into law. The final legislation, covering more than two hundred thousand domestic workers, mandates eight-hour workdays, overtime pay, a minimum of twenty-four consecutive hours of rest per week, at least three paid days off per year, protection against discrimination and harassment, and workers' compensation insurance protection. The New York Domestic Workers' Bill of Rights became a flagship campaign, a symbol of the beginning of the end of invisibility for domestic workers around the country. The work in New York inspired women around the country who were part of the newly formed National Domestic Workers Alliance.

During the six years of the bill of rights campaign, on trips to Albany and in meetings with legislators, we came to understand the obstacles that stood between us and a legal acknowledgment of the value of domestic work. We realized we could not accomplish our goals with only the voices of this virtually invisible workforce. This led to a powerful, transformative shift in our organizing, as we understood that nearly everyone is connected to someone who works as a domestic worker, whether they were raised by a domestic worker or employed a worker, had relatives who were caregivers or themselves had done caregiving work. We learned that bringing domestic workers' experiences into the light formally also brought many domestic employers' struggles into the light as well. This enabled us to see the shared goals and potential power of our collaboration.

We could—and would—build a winning coalition that crossed lines of race, class, gender, and age, including other workers who were familiar with the situation of caregivers and interacted with our workforce everyday, such as members of the doormen's and security guards' union (SEIU Local 32BJ), workers who faced similar obstacles, such as farmworkers (also excluded from the protection of labor laws); and other leaders who had family members who were domestic workers (such as then president of the AFL-CIO, John Sweeney); as well as racial justice groups, immigrant groups, women's organizations, faith-based groups, students, and celebrities. Finally, and most powerful of all, were the children who were looked after by nannies, the elders and others who were supported by caregivers, and the people who employed those domestic workers.

Much of traditional labor organizing has been about seeing the boss as the enemy. Yet in the intimate space in which caregivers work, the "us versus them" model no longer serves. While there are often antagonisms in the employment relationship, there are also often deep ties of familiarity and affection between workers and the families they work with. Because of the nature of the work and the intimacy of the relationship between domestic employers and workers—sometimes these workers know their employers better than they know themselves—and the workers see the employers as human. Negotiations between the two parties are best when they strive for mutual benefit. The moment when employers of domestic workers became our partners was a profound step toward understanding how finding common ground—being able to see and take into account the other's experience—is critical for meaningful societal transformation.

The task of building a more caring economy and a caring nation means that we have to come together across differences in race, culture, class, and generations in ways that this country has never seen. This convergence is about embracing the full breadth of who we truly are and who we are becoming as a nation. We have to engage all of the communities that are impacted by the elder boom: care workers, senior groups, disability rights advocates, women's organizations, unions, communities of faith, youths, and students. This is the Caring Majority; the powerful intergenerational alignment of American experiences that represent the full diversity of who we are as a nation, with unlimited potential to change the political landscape, and the basic value that connects us all: care.

I believe we have a Caring Majority in the United States; it's who we are—who we were meant to be—and it can provide the base of our power as we work together to create broad, accessible solutions that can work for all of us.

Three Fronts

Establishing the Caring Majority framework hadn't just built the short-term power we needed to win our legislative fight. In important ways, it began changing the nature of relationships, particularly the behavior of individual community members toward domestic workers. It also began the essential work of shifting popular culture toward noticing, appreciating, and valuing work that takes place in the home. The New York campaign proved that in order to transform our nation into a caring nation, we are going to need to create change in three arenas of society: cultural, behavioral, and structural.

We can sometimes forget that deep, lasting change requires work on all three of these fronts. For example, as part of a larger strategy for deep social change, the civil rights movement had a clear agenda for legislative change: to end the racial segregation that was established by law in the southern United States. And the movement was successful: restaurants and buses were desegregated, African Americans won the right to vote in the South, and more. Some people thought the movement for racial equality could and would end with the passage of the Civil Rights Act, but it continues today.

In fact, schools are *more* segregated now than they were in the 1960s,[1] and housing segregation is also on the rise.[2] We are still fighting racism on the level of individual interactions, whether it's the racial profiling by individual police officers or the tragic killing of Trayvon Martin by George Zimmerman in 2013, and the institutions, such as the court system, that reinforce these individual actions. Racial inequality is so deeply embedded in U.S. society that it will take a holistic approach to social change to undo it. To manifest the vision of the civil rights movement, we need ongoing strategies that address the ways that racial inequality continues to underlie and shape government policies and the economy, strategies that understand that today's racism plays out in different ways than it did in the 1960s, some less obvious. And we need to keep challenging the cultural assumptions and behavioral patterns that continue to divide us from one another.

The women's movement in the 1960s and 1970s gives us another powerful example of an integrated approach to social change. While the women's movement won a number of important policy victories, its core platform—the Equal Rights Amendment, which would have amended the Constitution to ensure equal rights for women—failed to pass. But even with this political defeat, the social and cultural efforts of the women's movement have radically changed our society. Today, women are doing things that would have been unimaginable just half a century ago. Cultural change was at the heart of those structural changes.

These two movements saw the work to win equality as a long-term process. Their leaders knew that they had to work on all three fronts if they were going to make progress. That is the approach we need to take if we are going to find our way to a new era of caring in America.

To change culture, we must tap into a more human story about what's happening in the world and why, one that works to shift attitudes, values, and identities and open up a more complex and complete picture. Who are today's elders? How is that changing? What is women's work in this era? How are we experiencing care, and how do we value the work of providing care? How do we picture immigrants? Who are our caring heroes? Working in the cultural arena taps into our emotional life in ways that move our hearts and minds, which are fundamental to making lasting progress.

A second arena of societal change is behavioral and relational. This is where we support shifts in the actions of individual people, families, or groups of people. What can families do to strengthen intergenerational bonds? What conversations should family members have? What can neighbors, friends, and communities do to provide elders with dignity and security? This work is about creating the opportunity for people to transform their practices and relationships with one another.

The third and final arena is structural or policy change, where we set or influence political agendas, gain the representation of politicians, change or implement public policies, or build new systems and institutions. These public policies might determine resource allocation, for example, in the budget process, or specify the inclusion, exclusion, regulation, or protection of certain populations, activities, or resources. What kinds of institutions can we build to support elders, families, and caregivers? What is the most effective role for federal and state agencies in supporting caregiving? How can we pay for care work, even while individual families are stuck in dire economic situations?

Whether it's taking the initiative to have difficult conversations with family members, strengthening communication with our paid caregivers, or getting involved in advocating for policy change, every arena holds an invitation for people to get involved and help build a society that recognizes the role of care in living out our lives with dignity.

The C

What   come to mind when we think of growi   in faces we easily generate: the ample   aking cookies for her grandkids, the v   nbers what younger generations have forg   tesman who advises his younger colleagues, even the man who sleeps under the overpass, or the lonely woman at the nursing home yearning to share her stories with anyone, and more. We might not think about Eve, the eighty-two-year-old surfer in Malibu, or the fact that many older actors are at the peak of their careers, experiencing new visibility with age and grace. How do we think about our elders, or do we think about them at all? Does the way we think of aging make us terrified of reaching old age ourselves?

As for caregivers, do we picture them as competent, bright individuals who navigate the complex terrain of family dynamics with sensitivity and humor? Or do we think, as Marlene and Erlinda said, that they just "clean toilets" and "wipe ass"? Do we consider them professionals? Do we even think of them at all? Do we appreciate our family caregivers—our mothers, sisters, grandmothers, fathers—for their hard work and sacrifice? Would we encourage our youth to pursue a career in caregiving?

In order to achieve a future with dignity, we must achieve a profound cultural shift in how most Americans feel about aging and care. That involves joining the national conversations in the news and in advertising, online, in films, and on TV and radio, all of which "affect how young people anticipate their future and how they interact with older people, and on the other hand, influence the way older people participate socially and evaluate their potential and limitations," according to the International Longevity Center.[3] Since boomers are the first generation of Americans who grew up with television—witnessing historic events like the moonwalk, the Vietnam War, and the assassinations of John F. Kennedy and Martin Luther King Jr. there—they are particularly influenced by what television says about aging. (Or by what it doesn't say: elder characters and actors, especially those over the age of eighty, are so underrepresented they're nearly invisible.)

Hollywood and the mainstream media are already beginning to reflect a sea change in how we understand aging, intergenerational relationships, and caregiving. Probably the single most effective product to come out of Hollywood in terms of turning around the cultural stereotypes about older women was the hugely popular and successful television show *The Golden Girls* in the late 1980s and early 1990s. Those four women, each with her own distinct history and personality (Blanche! Rose!), shattered the silence and the invisibility around aging in the most hilarious and endearing ways. It's high time someone takes up the mantle and continues telling vibrant, complex stories about older people, especially in a world where there are more elder consumers of culture than ever before. I think of the scene in *The Best Exotic Marigold Hotel*, where a group of British retirees converge on a retirement property in India, and luminous older actor Judi Dench's character proclaims, "This is a new and different world. The challenge is to cope with it. Not just cope but thrive."

Our new stories about care and aging must be told so that many different kinds of people can relate to them on an emotional level. We need more complex, diverse elder characters and caregiving characters. As we depict more older people and caregivers, we will be able to see the world through their eyes. Removing their invisibility will be a huge relief for younger and middle-age adults also, who consciously or unconsciously are plagued with unease about their own late years.

Dealing with Death

Our fear of dying obliterates every other fear, but our culture gives us little opportunity to confront and deal with it. The fear of death is understandable: death is frightening, sad, and overwhelming. But it is also inevitable, and ignoring death isn't doing anyone any good.

People with fatal illnesses often talk about how painful and lonely it is to have accepted their own death, while friends and family are so uncomfortable with the prospect that they can't even be around the dying person. But avoiding a dying person deprives us of one of the most meaningful opportunities in life: to get closure and say good-bye. Sometimes it takes losing someone suddenly, without a chance to take our leave, to understand how important it is to acknowledge the dying before they leave us.

Recently I've experienced not one but three untimely deaths of friends around my age. One of them was Becky Tarbotton. I met Becky in a yearlong leadership training program. She was relatively new in her role as director of the Rainforest Action Network, a global nonprofit organization that advocates for the protection of our planet's rain forests and the communities who live in them. As another thirtysomething woman newly leading an organization with a mission to address one of the great intractable problems of our time, she was a source of hope and inspiration for me. I was particularly moved by the ways she pushed through difficult times with humor, optimism, and her easygoing San Francisco style. Becky was a great storyteller. She played the fiddle.

I learned of Becky's passing on December 27, 2012. I was at the dinner table when I got a call from our mutual friend Ben. He said, "I have some sad news. It's Becky. She passed away." I could barely hear his voice, it was so quiet. I thought maybe I heard wrong; in a panic I got loud. "What?! What do you mean? What are you talking about? I don't believe you . . ." The day before, Becky had been on the beach with her new husband and friends. She got caught in the waves, and she made it to shore but ultimately didn't survive. The coroner ruled the cause of death as asphyxiation from the water she inhaled while swimming.

She was thirty-nine and so alive. It seemed impossible that she could be dead. She had been in her role as the executive director of the Rainforest Action Network for just two years. She had married the love of her life the previous year.

I grieved Becky's loss differently than I grieved the loss of my grandfather or other much older people who have passed. Becky's loss felt violent, violating, and was accompanied by a feeling of loss about what this young person could have offered the world for so many years to come, and what the sudden loss meant for her partner and parents. Days after hearing the news and understanding it on a cognitive level, my body still could not accept that she was no longer with us; I felt physically sick every time I saw a photograph of her or thoughts of her entered my mind. I understood the term "heartbreak" in a new, visceral way.

While grappling with these nearly incapacitating emotions, those of us Becky had loved and left behind also had to deal with some practical issues, like what to do with Becky's Facebook profile. Someone discovered Modern Loss, a website with resources and personal essays about grieving and loss for and by the "online generation," created by two thirtysomething women. It feels promising that a straightforward, accessible website about death and loss like this exists, part of the cultural shift we need to make as a nation.

Modern Loss isn't the only sign I see of the beginnings of a cultural shift around the subject of dying. I notice more and more people having much more productive, open, and transformative conversations and experiences around death and dying.

For example, over the past two decades there's been a dramatic increase in the number of medical schools integrating a death-and-dying curriculum. There was the very popular HBO series *Six Feet Under*, a typical family drama show . . . except that the family business happened to be running a funeral home. Seeing a family so constantly surrounded by death—even though here dealing with death was the family profession—opened the door for viewers to also confront mortality.

In my own personal discovery process following Becky's death, I felt the sharp pain of those early days and weeks gradually subside. I had no choice but to join with all the beloveds she had left behind and celebrate her life: all the ways she loved, risked, fought, played, and lived fully. Today, I can mostly smile thinking about her and her own mischievous smile. Coming around to an acceptance of Becky's death and an appreciation of her time on earth was a kind of gift. I learned the critical silver lining of death: the deepest gratitude and appreciation for the time we have together and our shared experiences.

For many people, death has been reduced to biological circumstances around the end of a body's functioning, and the fact that more and more people are dying in hospitals just underscores this. Yet death is really a human event, a social event. We know that the best situation for passing from life involves not medicine or medical technologies, but being surrounded by loved ones at home or in a comfortable environment, able to get closure in important relationships and be free from pain and regrets.

The Buddhist teacher and nun Pema Chödrön writes that "we are raised in a culture that fears death and hides it from us. Nevertheless, we experience it all the time. We experience it in the form of disappointment, in the form of things not working out.

We experience it in the form of things always being in a process of change. When the day ends, when the second ends, when we breathe out, that's death in everyday life." [4] That means we have endless moments to practice letting go, to learn about grieving, and to prepare for death. We can use every passing sunset and season as an opportunity to rehearse. We prepare so extensively and with so much love for birth in our families and homes, but for the miracle of death, we rarely prepare at all.

Late-Life Purpose

Another conversation we need to have in America is about the value of a person's contributions to society after retirement. Both America's "Protestant work ethic" and the mystique around self-reliance and independence mean that retirement is often interpreted as a loss of status. Yet there are so many opportunities for elders to continue to make meaningful, substantial contributions, regardless of their formal status as retired. I'm not even talking about the vague notion of "wisdom": the possession of enormous institutional knowledge and know-how in workplaces and communities. Certainly, some of an elder's experience becomes obsolescent (in certain fields, especially), but much of it remains entirely relevant to work performance and outputs.

In fact, there's a group called the Elders, founded by Nelson Mandela in 2007 at the urging of entrepreneur Richard Branson and musician Peter Gabriel, that brings together retired global leaders to work together for peace and human rights. Its members include former UN secretary-general and Nobel Peace Laureate Kofi Annan (born 1938), former U.S. president Jimmy Carter (born 1924), former Irish president Mary Robinson (born

1944), Nobel Peace Laureate Desmond Tutu (born 1931), and Ela Bhatt, founder of the more than one-million-strong Self-Employed Women's Association in India (born 1933). Having "earned international trust, demonstrated integrity and built a reputation for inclusive, progressive leadership," the Elders use "their collective influence to open doors and gain access to decision makers."[5]

Similar occupations for which less famous older people are well suited include supervising, coaching, teaching, creating long-term strategies, and synthesizing data from interdisciplinary sources or from across history. There's a wonderful project called Encore.org that connects retirees with "encore careers—jobs that combine personal meaning, continued income and social impact" in public sector or nonprofit work, and promotes the work of extraordinary encore careerists by handing out the annual Purpose Prize, a $100,000 award.[6] One Purpose Prize winner in 2010 was Inez Killingsworth, who worked past her seventy-fifth birthday. Until she passed away in 2013, Inez led an organization that fights foreclosures in Ohio, testifying in front of Congress, taking bank executives on tours of the ruins of foreclosed houses and getting them to promise to stop shady mortgage practices, and helping thousands of families each year stay in their homes.[7] In 2014, Barbara Young, nanny and caregiver from Barbados and longtime leader in our organization, received a Purpose Prize for her contributions to securing rights and recognition for domestic workers in an "encore" role as worker organizer.

Another notable shift is the increasing role that elders are playing in child care. As more and more women enter the workforce, and more households are dual income, grandparents and older neighbors provide experienced, motivated, high-quality care.

Grandparents usually love their grandchildren to pieces, and vice versa. Grandparental involvement in raising children strengthens intergenerational relationships. And in some communities, significant numbers of grandparents have become the primary caregivers for their grandchildren. I'm thinking particularly of children whose parents have been incarcerated or deported or whose parents have faced long-term unemployment and been forced to migrate long distances in search of work.

We're already seeing the beautiful impacts of more grandparental involvement in raising younger generations. The Pew Research Center says 16 percent of all American homes now house multiple generations, up from 12 percent in the 1980s, while among Latino, African American, and Asian families this trend is especially prevalent, with at least 40 percent living in households with three generations.[8] A report from Pew Research Social and Demographic Trends on Millennials found: "They respect their elders. A majority say that the older generation is superior to the younger generation when it comes to moral values and work ethic. Also, more than six-in-ten say that families have a responsibility to have an elderly parent come live with them if that parent wants to. By contrast, fewer than four-in-ten adults ages 60 and older agree that this is a family responsibility."[9]

One way communities are beginning to lift up the role of grandparents is by expanding our society's celebrations of National Grandparents Day. Most Americans aren't even aware this official holiday exists. Yet it has been around since 1978, falling on the first Sunday after Labor Day each year. In 2013, to help celebrate it, Caring Across Generations encouraged people to share stories about their grandparents on Twitter with the hashtag #granecdote. Celebrity ambassadors led the way, and we reached more than 4 million people, showing our grandparents some love. Hopefully, this will have marked just the beginning of our national love affair with our grandparents.

The Behavior Shift

Our metamorphosis into a caring society also happens on the level of relationships, inside families, within neighborhoods, with people we see and interact with every day. It begins with respectful communication in our own homes. Everyone spends time listening as well as speaking: spouses with each other; adult children with their aging parents and with their siblings; sandwich generation adults with both their children and their parents; care recipients—employers—with their caregiving employees; professional caregivers with other caregivers; elders with other elders; neighbors across generations; new immigrants with established citizens; and so on, in every permutation. When we communicate effectively and listen well, we remove the fear that comes from not knowing the other and the other's situation. We put ourselves in the shoes of the other, and we take better care of one another.

Talking with children, parents, partners, siblings, and other relatives about how everyone envisions their life in later years—and their death—cannot start early enough. Discussions about aging and death need to become simply a part of the fabric of family life. When I asked Robin—the sandwich generation mother of teenagers and also an adult daughter caring for her dad with Parkinson's—about her advice for fellow members of the sandwich generation, she immediately responded, "It's really important that you are able to talk with your parents. In families where parents keep secrets or children don't ask questions, it creates a lot of problems."

Conversations between the family members hiring a professional caregiver and the caregiving employee are equally important. When the National Domestic Workers Alliance interviewed hundreds of employers of domestic workers, one employer with a strong relationship with her domestic employee said, "We spend a lot of time talking about our personal lives. I know way more about her than I know about a lot of my colleagues with whom I work. Her son is going through a lot and we spent a lot of time talking about him." As with family conversations, patience, respect, and good listening are key to both sides understanding each other's needs and expectations.

Nikki Brown-Booker is a licensed marriage and family therapist in California who has had disabilities her whole life and began hiring personal attendants at the age of eighteen when she moved out of her parents' house. She works full-time and plays an active role in her community with the assistance of a team of six personal attendants. She handles their hiring (and firing) and supervision and says about the relationships with her employees: "I have developed strong, important relationship with many of my attendants. They are mothers, college students, wives, and sometimes grandparents, and they have lives outside of my life that they are struggling with. I know that when I am treated fairly and respectfully at my own work, I do a better job, and the same is true of all workers. I believe that my employees deserve to have a workplace that they feel comfortable in and that they are treated with respect. I believe all attendants deserve good treatment, fair wages, and decent benefits including paid sick days." [10]

Both sides often feel uncomfortable and anxious about subjects like money, immigration status, and formalizing the terms of employment. Many employers feel awkward about the inherent power dynamic in the employment relationship; they don't necessarily feel comfortable wielding that type of power. Because of the ways that racial segregation continues to shape our society, the caregiver may be the only person from another racial background in the employer's life. This can lead to miscommunication and awkwardness in conversations about employment issues, so many people try to avoid these conversations altogether. These dynamics can be compounded by language differences. But it is better to be honest about the power imbalances and the miscommunications and the moments of awkwardness and to work through them. If we avoid them, they don't go away. They stay around, and they keep us alienated from each other. Employers and caregivers have come together in cities around the country to develop healthier ways of interacting with each other on the job. There are resources for negotiations between employers and paid caregivers in Appendix B.

It is important to bring all the people involved in elder caregiving into the same room, so we can learn about one another's experiences and come to understand one another more deeply. Jews for Racial and Economic Justice in New York City started a series of events bringing together caregivers and older adults in one community to share perspectives and develop a common vision for healthy caregiving relationships called the Eldercare Dialogues. The organization's director, Marjorie Dove Kent, describes a scene in a packed room at Congregation B'nai Jeshurun on Manhattan's Upper West Side:

At the center of the room sits a circle of eight people. All eyes are on them. They are telling stories about death, about the moment when a person who they supported in life passed away. For some, a spouse or a parent. For others, an employer. One woman talks about the moment her employer of many years, an 86-year-old man, died in her arms. Crying, she tells the room about her profound honor in helping her dear employer move gracefully out of this life. Translators provide simultaneous interpretation.

The next speaker talks through her shame, describing the last days of her mother's life, how when she moved her mother into a hospital, she discontinued all communication with her mother's live-in home care attendant, even when the worker tried to find out where she could visit her former patient. The speaker hadn't realized, she said, the depth of the relationship that forms between an elder and the person who supports them most intimately in those final years of life.

The room breathes a collective sigh as the speakers take a break. At the tables, seniors and their family members admit the isolation they've been feeling, and their fearfulness about who will be there for them or their parents at the end. Home care workers see themselves in these stories, and reflect on their own fears, both for their employment and their own aging and end-of-life care.[11]

Hundreds of caregivers, seniors, and their family members have participated in these community conversations, a great model for congregations and community centers across the country. My goal is for a million conversations like these to take place in neighborhoods around the country in the coming years, to weave us together in the shared identity of the Caring Majority: people from all walks of life having courageous conversations with loved ones about our visions of care in the future.

Neighbors Forge Solutions

In the absence of comprehensive nationwide eldercare programs, many people are developing their own solutions by gathering with friends and neighbors to meet their needs. American communities are experimenting with makeshift solutions to create and sustain the quality of life they feel they deserve. In *Passages in Caregiving*, Gail Sheehy writes, "Aging in community means meeting new friends and getting discounts—from hairdressers to personal trainers to massage therapy, all the way to home care [and] meal deliveries. . . . I think of it as a resurgence of the commune spirit of the 1960s. Instead of isolation, aging boomers want to belong to communal families, networked as part of a virtual community, with a spicy variety of ages, sexes, cultural backgrounds and life experiences." [12]

One example of a community-based response is Naturally Occurring Retirement Communities (NORCs). Not created with the intention of housing or serving senior citizens, instead these are neighborhoods and housing developments where many people who settled some time ago have now grown old and retired. NORCs tend to develop in one of three ways: a large number of people moved into a community when they were younger and aged in place; a large number of seniors migrated to a neighborhood, despite it not being specifically intended to serve elderly residents; or a large number of younger residents in a community moved away, leaving a majority of elders. A NORC with a Supportive Service Program typically offers health care management, education, recreation, and volunteer opportunities. Some also offer adult day care, meals, transportation, home care, legal and financial advice, and home modifications.

Victor Quintana lives in a NORC in Upper Manhattan, New York. He and his wife bought their apartment in an affordable housing development in 1995, unaware of the retirement community that was developing there among seniors who had previously settled there and aged over time. It was when his wife's parents moved into the development in 2005 that the existence—and the benefits—of the NORC became clear to him. His wife's father had Alzheimer's before passing away, and her mother is recovering from hip surgery. The NORC's relationship with Mount Sinai Medical Center offers residents access to one of the best programs for older people's medical and mental health.

For National Grandparents Day, Victor says, the community screened a movie, hired a magician, and served cream puffs so that grandparents could offer their grandkids something memorable. Victor is retiring in August 2014 and is looking forward to becoming more active in the NORC because, he says, "As I've learned more about the program, I feel like . . . wow, this is a really good thing. It's not perfect, but the quality of the people, the values, the commitment to each other . . . We're lucky." [13]

Another phenomenon since the early 2000s, Villages have emerged as an innovative model to help people remain in their homes and connect with their communities throughout later life. The idea of a Village is that neighbors help neighbors as much as they can. Villages are self-governing, grassroots, community-based organizations that coordinate access to a variety of supportive services to promote aging in place, social integration, health, and well-being. As of 2012 there were 85 Villages across the country, with 120 more in development.[14]

Typically there is a small (often just one person) paid staff who organizes activities and transportation and who manages the "front desk," where members can request services. Members also volunteer to provide services to other members, such as offering rides or organizing social events. Some services—such as health and personal care, housekeeping, legal assistance—tend to be provided by external "preferred providers," whose services are vetted by the Village and sometimes discounted for Village members. Villages are mostly funded by membership fees, in addition to donations. For example, at Beacon Hill Village in Boston, the first Village established in the country, membership costs $600 per year for an individual, or $890 for a couple, although about 30 percent of the Village's members who have annual incomes of between $45,000 and $50,000 receive a reduced membership rate. Beacon Hill's 450 members, aged between their fifties and hundreds, can rely on prescreened and often discounted service providers including carpenters and plumbers, chefs and computer technicians, and home health aides and caregivers, all just a phone call away.

At ninety, Chicago native Maurine Phinisee can get around her home on Capitol Hill in Washington, D.C., on her own, but she needs help opening jars, reaching things in high places, repairing things around the house, and driving around town. She manages because she lives in Capitol Hill Village.

"I came [to D.C.] because Eleanor Roosevelt, the wife of Franklin D. Roosevelt, sent out cards to people, girls, women, all over the United States to come and help the war effort in Washington. So, I became a government girl," she told the Capitol Hill History Project in an interview. "On April 11, 1942, I boarded the B&O Columbian train at 3:30 pm. It was scheduled to arrive in Washington, DC at 8:30 am on April 12. And that's when I got here. April 12, 1942." [15]

Today, a half century later, if she needs someone to weed her garden, fix a broken window, or drive her to the store, she calls the Village office and they send someone. When possible, they send volunteers, other Capitol Hill Village members, like Ed and Margaret Missiaen, who are in their late sixties. Margaret works in Phinisee's garden, and Ed, a former Peace Corps volunteer who retired from the U.S. Department of Agriculture in 1997, has helped fix her windows. Ed has also served as the treasurer of the Capitol Hill Village. His biography reads, "He can be found these days changing light bulbs all around the neighborhood."

In the last decade, writes Gail Sheehy, "the village movement has substantially changed the way many seniors think about preserving their independence and replenishing their sense of belonging as they move past sixty-five into their seventies and eighties." [16]

Meanwhile, in Japan, another community-based program has become widely embraced as a unique cost-saving strategy that simultaneously builds community: a caregiving time bank. Essentially, people can provide care for elders and receive an electronic credit that is paid into a computerized savings account. The "time dollar" alternative currency is called the Fureai Kippu, which translates as "Caring Relationship Tickets." Each unit in Fureai Kippu is an hour of service, but different rates apply to different services (e.g., one hour of reading is credited with one Fureai

Kippu, while help with bathing is valued at two Fureai Kippu for each hour of service). These Fureai Kippu can be saved for the individual's own use in the future or transferred to someone of their choice, typically a parent or family member who lives elsewhere in the country and who needs similar assistance.

The system reduces costs in several ways, for example, by postponing expensive retirement homes as well as reducing recovery time in hospitals after a medical procedure. The resources sidestep government subsidies, bureaucracy, and expensive insurance, instead flowing directly and efficiently from one member of the community to the next. Elders who have been surveyed have consistently said they preferred services provided by people paid in Fureai Kippu over those paid in yen.

Bernard Lietaer, author of *Access to Human Wealth: Money Beyond Greed and Scarcity* described the system:

It makes it possible for hundreds of thousands of [elderly] people to stay in their homes much longer than they otherwise could. Otherwise, you'd have to put most of these people into a home for seniors, which costs an arm and a leg to society, and they're unhappy there. So nobody's winning. . . .

"Time dollars" help in a lot of communities where conventional money is scarce: in ghettos, retirement communities, high unemployment zones, student communities. . . .

These are places where people are likely to have more time than money. Rather than competing in a competitive market where dollars are exchanged, they share services in a co-operative market where they help each other.[17]

The closest thing we have to Japan's Fureai Kippu system in the United States is a pilot program based in New York City called Caring Collaborative.[18] The program organizes its members by zip code and sets up a time-bank system so people can provide care for one another in emergencies or during illness.

One last community-based idea that we've dreamed up that has yet to be implemented is currently known as Care to Own. Imagine four two-bedroom apartments, grouped around a shared garden, called a "carepod." Were it to be viewed from above, a carepod would resemble a plus sign, with green at its center. Each apartment in the carepod belongs to a caregiver, who hosts an elder or person needing care. Each caregiver is called a host, while the person she or he cares for is called a guest. The elder—the guest—lives on the garden level, while the caregiver lives upstairs in a fully contained unit. Ideally, these carepods are situated within diverse communities full of families and singles of all ages, with easy access to public transit, shops, and other urban or suburban infrastructure.

To become a host, a caregiver has to provide an initial $5,000 to enroll, as a sign of good faith. The guest, who has his or her own bedroom and bathroom, might pay $2,000 per month for being there, for twenty-four-hour proximity to supervision and assistance as well as all meals: that's very competitive with nursing home care, if not very low. Every month, half of that fee is automatically deposited toward the mortgage of the caregiver's unit, coming to $12,000 per year in this scenario. If each apartment in the carepod is worth $150,000, that means that after roughly fifteen years, the host's mortgage will be paid off.

Hosts therefore make a fifteen-year commitment to the program, with the one stipulation that the guest unit must always be occupied by a paying person in need of care. After the fifteen years, a host can cash out (take their $150,000 and buy a house somewhere, retire, or return to their country of origin) or stay longer; once the mortgage has been paid off, the host receives the full monthly payment from the guest.

Carepod hosts are motivated to take good care of the property because it belongs to them. Because the units are arranged in pods of four, hosts can support one another or swap duties to allow one another to take time off—they *careshare* with one another to make life easier. The elders—the guests—should also develop meaningful, fun, supportive relationships with the three others who live inside the same carepod, as well as with others in the neighborhood. This sharing model alleviates pressure on hosts, freeing them up as often as is feasible, depending on the intensity of the care required by their guests. The carepod structure and careshare arrangement also mean that each group of four hosts helps hold one another accountable for being the best caregivers they can be.

As we seek to support our elders in aging at home and maintaining relationships in their communities, these are models to keep in mind. They are powerful reminders of what we can build when we communicate effectively and work collectively. We can always choose to prioritize care. There are many things we can do that strengthen community and build interdependence across differences of age, background, and belief.

However, while much has been built on the initiative and creativity of individuals and families, neighbors and communities, without waiting for elected officials to pass public policy, each of these innovations would be greatly supported by public policy. When these initiatives are linked together, fortified by a new, more visible and dignified culture around aging and caring, and supported by an integrated public system—that's when the change in any one person's backyard transforms into a national solution.

"I support her in the small things that make up her daily routine. I feel good caring for her; she's very sweet," says Miriam, also a graduate of the adult care training program at the women's organization Mujeres Unidas y Activas in the Bay Area. For more than twenty years, Mujeres Unidas y Activas has advocated for women in the immigrant community. PHOTOGRAPH BY ALESSANDRA SANGUINETTI

5

A POLICY OF CARING

A healthy social life is found
When in the mirror of each human soul
The whole community is shaped,
And when in the community
Lives the strength of each human soul.
                                    —Rudolf Steiner

Once upon a time, toward the end of the nineteenth century, as rail travel for the first time enabled regular land transport of people and goods over long distances, the U.S. government realized that railroads were a sink-or-swim proposition. There was no keeping up with the global pace of industry and development without them. So our government gave away more than 100 million acres in land grants—greater than the size of California—for the development of railroads. Congress authorized loans—between $10,000 and $50,000 per mile of railroad, depending on the difficulty of the terrain—to assist with construction. A little more than half a century later, President Eisenhower devoted the unheard-of sum of $25 billion to the creation of 41,000 miles of interstate highway system—at the time, the largest public works project in history.

And when in the 1880s electricity became an even more fundamental prerequisite to modern life than railroads, it was first the private utilities, like Thomas Edison's, that began wiring and powering cities. But while New York, Chicago, and other cities enjoyed electric light and early labor-saving devices like sewing machines, rural America was in the dark. The only light after sundown came from smoky, dangerous lamps. Every chore still required backbreaking manual labor. These farms were too far from the generators and too widely dispersed to be profitable to urban power companies. And so much of the country remained in the dark for decades.

But at the end of the Great Depression, President Franklin Delano Roosevelt saw the solution to this hardship as an opportunity to create jobs and stimulate manufacturing. On May 11, 1935, as part of the New Deal, he signed an executive order establishing the Rural Electrification Administration, which provided loans and other assistance so that rural cooperatives—groups of farmers—could build and run their own electrical distribution systems. Within two years the program brought electricity to some 1.5 million farms through 350 rural cooperatives in forty-five states. Almost half of all farms were wired by 1942, with the remainder following by the 1950s.

And then there was the case of the Internet, pieces of which were originally developed by and for the Defense Department, as well as universities and other research institutions in the 1960s and 1970s. Over subsequent decades, government invested in the research and development as well as physical infrastructure for the technologies that would become today's Internet, arguably as fundamental and significant a component of modern life and commerce as electricity.

Over and over again, at key turning points, we have invested in the infrastructure needed to thrive as a nation and to lead the safe, productive, and fulfilling lives that as individual Americans we expect to live. And over and over again, these big ideas, and the momentum behind them, not only transformed our lives but also transformed our economy. In fact, in many cases, these investments *were* our economy, and most certainly saved our economy.

An infrastructure for care may seem different from an infrastructure for railroads, highways, electricity, or the Internet. There are no trees to clear or wires to lay. Yet care is among the fundamental building blocks of society. For any of us, thinking of our most basic needs—care always comes first. There's no need for the Internet, or even electricity, if there's no way to feed, bathe, or clothe yourself.

Since care is a need that's shared across American families, it should be a responsibility that's shared by all of us as a nation. We brought water, electricity, and the Internet to every home. We can bring quality care to every home. But the Care Grid is a system we're going to have to invest in and create together. When we build the infrastructure we need to support human life, so much energy will be released in positive, transformative ways in our families, community, and economy. Rather than each of us struggling through in lonely isolation, we will have a shared base of support and structure on which to build our individual lives. As the elder boom arrives, we must take up the building of a Care Grid. We've done it before, and we can do it again.

Evolution of Work and Technology

Every previous nationwide infrastructure we've built has involved a massive amount of ambition and creativity that often corresponds to leaps forward in technology and social innovation. The Care Grid is no exception.

For example, we know that new technologies can play a huge role in helping us improve the lives of elders, especially if we get involved in shaping their development. Already there are cars that drive themselves and wearable GPS systems that can help us keep track of loved ones with dementia. Maybe the future of care will involve robots like Paro, which looks like a baby seal and is designed to calm patients with dementia and Alzheimer's. Or perhaps butler-style robots will be available to offer reminders and fetch objects.

Then there's Betty, a tablet-based application developed by Robert Nascenzi, former CEO of a technology company called Nliven Systems, after he saw the messy three-ring binder that various aides were using to track his elderly mother's medications, doctor's appointments, and activities. Joan Gage, aka the Rolling Crone, who writes about technology and life after sixty, describes the device:

> When a home health caregiver checks into a patient's home, she can tap information about the patient into the tablet, describing what the patient ate, what activity he/she did, the patient's mood, any problems, medicines administered, doctors' appointments—information which is transmitted in real time to the patient's doctor and all family members who are subscribers to the plan. They can

receive this information with a smartphone application, or as text or email messages. (In addition to tapping, the tablet understands written messages or even voice recognition.) Subscribers can also respond and send private messages to agency staff through the Betty web portal. This way a patient's children can keep daily track of their elderly parents, no matter how far away, and a continuous record of the patient's condition and care plan is created.[1]

There is tremendous, well-founded concern that new technologies will replace significant numbers of workers at an economic moment when too many people are unemployed, and we simply could not afford that. While I strongly doubt that robots or other technologies will ever be able to fully replace human caregivers, it's exciting to imagine how a device such as the Betty tablet-based application could make a huge difference in the quality of life of elders, their families, and their professional caregivers. The goals and values driving innovation define their outcome. In this case, the goals should be better care and better jobs.

Meanwhile, deep shifts are also happening around the concept of work itself. On the one hand, most new jobs are low-wage jobs—for example, those associated with growth in farming, food service, personal care, building and grounds maintenance, and health care support—which have kept people living in poverty or on the brink.

On the other hand, we are also seeing a growing percentage of today's workforce becoming self-employed, temporary, or contract—so-called contingent work—as employers respond to economic uncertainties by choosing to "maintain workforce flexibility." And we're seeing a rise in the number of freelancers—generally a term applied to independent white-collar workers, often in creative or tech-related fields. By their sheer numbers they are attracting attention to the particular concerns of independent workers, which also benefits more marginalized workers. Across all fields, many independent workers are now coming together in new alliances, associations, unions, and worker-owned cooperatives or hiring halls where workers can set standards for wages and working conditions in this new economic environment.

For example, domestic workers have partnered with workers from eight other low-wage work sectors to form the United Workers Congress. The congress supports workers in organizing and leveraging their shared power to achieve higher wages and improved job quality. The eight sectors include guest workers, day laborers, tipped minimum-wage workers (such as restaurant workers), African American workers in the South, where worker protections are particularly weak and segregation is still widespread, farmworkers, taxi drivers, formerly incarcerated workers, and workfare workers (those doing unpaid work or training while receiving public assistance).

Cooperatives are another positive phenomenon emerging in many fields. In home care, the best model we have was born in the South Bronx, with an enterprise that began in 1985 called Cooperative Home Care Associates (CHCA). The worker-owned agency generates nearly $60 million annually in revenue and employs more than 2,050 staff, nearly all Latina and African American women, making it the largest worker-owned cooperative in the United States. CHCA employees are offered full-time hours, competitive wages, overtime paid at time-and-a-half of base wage, worker ownership, peer mentoring, financial literacy training, and supervision that balances coaching, support, and accountability. As a result, their annual turnover rate is half the industry average. Their model was adopted in the eastern part of the state of Wisconsin, where a worker-owned cooperative called Cooperative Care now provides in-home services for elderly residents of rural communities. According to a report by a regional Rural Health Research Center, not a single worker has left the co-op since it was started in 2001. That speaks volumes about the potential of cooperatives to vastly improve the experience of workers. Importantly, these co-ops are often involved in advocacy, bringing the voices of these workers to the table for policy making.

In Boston, a Brazilian American women's green-cleaning cooperative called Vida Verde, whose members make their own cleaning products out of natural, nontoxic ingredients, have agreed among themselves not to charge below a certain amount to clean houses, so that they all support one another to earn a decent, dignified living. Other co-ops train their members in negotiation, so that they can ask their employers for better wages and working conditions with confidence.

Sara Horowitz, founder of the Freelancers Union and a long-time friend of mine, is optimistic about the wave of independent and marginalized workers coming together like this in associations, unions, and cooperatives, describing it as the "New Mutualism": a reprise of the vibrant movement in the 1800s when American workers united to own cooperative local businesses, updated with today's connectivity of the Internet and mobile technology.

These collective efforts on the part of workers, including freelancers, recognize the changing nature of work and the opportunity to shape the future. Technology and innovation are driving change, but the values that guide innovation matter. Will robots replace and displace care workers, or will they offer relief and support workers to provide better quality care with less stress? And as more people work in part-time or self-employed contexts, will we create a new safety net that catches everyone, regardless of how their employment is structured? These are key questions for the care workforce and many other nontraditional workers whose arrangements have become the new normal.

Care work is such a significant part of the workforce of the future that it can become a model for the rest of the economy, with tremendous ripple effects. It can be a place where we attempt to leverage technology and innovation to pave a road from low-wage, high-burnout work to good jobs with benefits and security. It can offer the context for discussing both the new freedoms that a freelance economy offers, and a new framework for security for the twenty-first century that accounts for the needs of working people universally, such as paid sick days, child care, health care, and home care. If we fail to do so, we will continue to accelerate the expansion of unsustainable, poverty-wage care work and, in turn, undermine our ability to provide quality care for the millions who are counting on it.

Inspiration from Everywhere

Alongside the groundbreaking initiatives workers are undertaking directly, which could blossom further with government supports, there is also tremendous creativity happening at the state level, especially in states where the elder boom arrived early.

For example, Hawaii is developing its own state social insurance program to support long-term care. Vermont also is considering incorporating long-term care benefits as part of its single-payer system. Minnesota is looking into a statewide Accountable Care Organization that will cover everyone and include long-term care benefits. An Accountable Care Organization creates an integrated system that connects different levels of health care, such as hospitals, clinics, and administrators, to provide coordinated care to Medicare patients and keep costs in check. When it provides high-quality care at lower cost, it receives a share in the savings it achieves for Medicare.

In Washington State, the home care training program run by the Service Employees International Union is the second-largest educational program in the state after the University of Washington, training forty thousand workers per year, with capacity in thirteen languages. Workers graduate with skills and capability to support people in a range of environments and spectrum of needs. They receive all the skills needed to build meaningful partnerships with the people they support and their families.

Many states and municipalities have already developed multi-stakeholder long-term care commissions. Incorporating the perspectives of families, consumers, workers, and experts in health care and gerontology, more than a dozen states are forming care commissions to study the issue and develop state-level solutions. These commissions are considering new ideas such as:

- The creation of consumer care teams that help to reduce avoidable emergency room visits, readmission rates, and nursing home placement
- Programs to support diverse consumers to receive culturally appropriate care from the growing number of immigrants

in the direct care workforce in ways that benefit our entire
health care system by reducing health disparities across patient populations
- Tax credits for private-pay employers who pay a living
wage

Many states are seeing the opportunity to develop new and
exciting models of multi-stakeholder collaboration, to expand
home care, boost the economy and create jobs, and create new
efficiencies in the health care delivery system. In the lean start-
up model, cities and states could receive federal support to bring
these stakeholders together to develop and test solutions. By
learning from states' ongoing initiatives, we will start to see the
models that can be scaled, save our system money, and create
good jobs for the care workforce and more choices for consumers. We will then begin to make out the contours of a federal
solution that could work for the future.

We can also look outside our borders for inspiration. For some
time now, other countries have been experiencing the moral di-
lemma and financial strain that comes when a large, growing
population of elders needs care. Thanks to a combination of low
fertility and low mortality, Japan is the world leader in its population of old people, with currently nearly a quarter of its population aged sixty-five or older. By 2030 Japan expects one-third of
its people to be over sixty-five. Western Europe is also aging,
with some countries, including Germany, already with more than
20 percent of their populations over the age of sixty-five. Pension
and health systems are straining to meet increasing costs related
to health and care, supported by a shrinking working-age population, in other words, a diminishing tax base.

We are fortunate here in the United States to be able to study the social and political choices these countries made in managing the shift. Our elder boom runs behind theirs, with one-sixth of our population due to reach the age of sixty-five by 2020. It was 1997 when Japan passed that threshold (approximately 16 percent of the population over sixty-five), and 1994 when Germany did; in both countries this demographic turning point resulted in legislation establishing universal long-term care insurance programs. Germany began implementing its program in 1995 and Japan in 2000, and both evaluated and made subsequent revisions and adjustments to the programs, which means these countries provide more than a decade's worth of outcomes we can study.

Both countries wound up adopting universal social insurance programs to provide long-term care, in which eligibility is based on functional need, not on income, assets, or the availability of family caregivers. Both countries had to win over opponents—not only those who objected to additional mandatory costs, but also those who feared the social upheaval and erosion of family values—overturning traditions in which family members are duty bound to provide care and nonfamily care is stigmatized. In Japan especially, it had always been the role of women, specifically daughters-in-law, to care for a family's elders. The country's feminists joined with its economists in supporting the plan to shift the burden of care work so women could enter the workforce.

When people turn sixty-five in Japan, they can apply for benefits, at which time they are given an assessment. If they need help, they are approved for one of six levels of care, which may include a range of services, from home-based help with cooking and dressing to residential respite, as well as permanent care. Benefits, which are capped, are intended to cover 90 percent of formal caregiving costs both in institutions and in the community; the remaining costs are borne by the elderly individuals and their families. In contrast, Germany's long-term care program provides universal coverage for people of all ages. Its benefits are basic, covering about 50 percent of the average cost of institutional care and home care, with individuals expected to bear their portion of the costs. The system is meant to encourage both family caregiving and paid, nonfamily care provided in the home and community.

Both countries have in place social safety nets to help low-income individuals with any costs not covered by their universal programs. Some types of benefits are high impact but relatively inexpensive to the system, such as adult day care; respite for family caregivers; information, counseling, and training for family caregivers; and social security tax credits for family caregiving.

Both countries conduct needs assessments at people's homes. Care managers put together individualized packages of care and track costs. The national eligibility standards are published, reviewed, and periodically updated as needed.

Adopted *during an economic recession*, half of Japan's system is funded by general revenue funding—taxes. The other half comes from premiums paid both by retirees and by all working adults over the age of forty—with their contributions split equally between themselves (employees) and their employers. Germany's system is funded wholly on premiums, required from all retirees and employees of any age, with contributions of the working population also split equally between employees and their employers.

Germans who can afford to may opt out of the public program so long as they get private insurance. Private long-term care insurance is strictly regulated by the government so that the benefits and costs are on par with the public program.

The business communities in both countries did initially oppose the mandatory contribution, as would certainly happen in the United States, but they didn't prevail. The result in both countries has been reduced pressure on their social assistance and health care budgets, as well as expansive growth in the private sector, which is the primary source for delivering long-term care services.

Analyzing the budgetary impact of the long-term care insurance system on social assistance spending in Germany, Mary Jo Gibson, a former senior policy advisor for AARP, writes:

> [Long-term care insurance] clearly reduced the level of dependence on social assistance by individuals. Today, about 5 percent of those who receive [long-term care] at home, and about 25 percent of those in institutions, require additional social assistance benefits. Prior to the introduction of [long-term care insurance], roughly 80 percent of those in need of care in nursing homes received social assistance. In addition, social assistance budgets have been spared expenditures of roughly $6 billion Euros annually due to [long-term care insurance]. . . . Since the introduction of the program, expenditures by the social assistance program for nursing home care have been reduced by roughly two-thirds.[2]

Subsequent reforms—in 2006 in Japan, in 2008 in Germany, and another round in 2012 for both countries—have tweaked the systems as needed. Japan's reforms have focused mostly on controlling spending and increasing contributions, while Germany's have expanded access to care and benefits, particularly to the growing population of people with dementia.

Their examples fill me with hope and ambition.

Making the Case

The urgent need for a comprehensive federal policy of caring is not just a moral but a practical and economic necessity as the aging of the baby boom generation causes the number of individuals in the United States who are sixty-five years of age or older to increase from 40 million to 70 million during the next twenty years. We know that 70 percent of individuals who are sixty-five years of age or older need some form of long-term services and supports. With the elder boom, the total number of individuals needing long-term care is projected to grow from 12 million to 27 million by 2050.

We cannot rely on institutions like nursing homes to provide the needed services and care, not only because nearly 90 percent of Americans want to age at home, but also because the cost of institutional care is astronomical: $84,000 per person per year, for thirty months, on average. Middle-class Americans are increasingly caught between two tiers of care depending upon income: Medicaid for the poor, often in nursing homes, and privately financed residential or home care for the wealthy, with wide disparities in access and quality.

In twenty-first-century America, with families' smaller size and greater mobility, along with more and more women working outside the home, relying on traditional unpaid caregiving by family members is not a viable solution. Aging at home necessitates home care workers. Yet the 3 million people currently in this workforce cannot even meet the needs now, let alone the needs when we have nearly twice as many elders. We will have to have at least 1.8 million additional home care workers in the next decade. Unless we ship those needing care overseas, home care jobs by their very nature cannot be outsourced, so this job growth is good news given ongoing unemployment and underemployment. Yet because these jobs are low status, with poor wages and benefits and high levels of hazards and stress, turnover among care workers is high, further exacerbating the need. Almost a quarter of today's home care workers were born outside the United States, which means that immigration issues also impact the workforce.

An early mentor of mine always said, "Wherever there is suffering, people will always work together to create solutions." And it is clear there is already great suffering on all sides of the care equation. Yet there will be much deeper anguish and suffering if we do not act now.

Policies for a Caring America

The Care Grid brings together public, private, and nonprofit resources and creates a comprehensive, coordinated system in which elders can age with dignity and their caregivers, both professional paid workers and unpaid family or friends, can thrive as well. The first elements of such a Care Grid are already in place. With some bold, clear-eyed restructuring of our priorities and budgets, we can build out a set of policies and infrastructure to enable us to live out our lives with dignity, no matter who we are, at any age.

The main goals of the policy change are clear. We know we need more jobs in home care. We know we need home care to be affordable, easily accessible, and delivered at the highest quality. We need these jobs to be well-respected and secure with living wages, benefits, security, and opportunities for career advancement. We need the workforce to be prepared, trained, and adaptive to the particular needs of the individuals and families they are supporting. And we need for everyone to feel like whole and equal parts of a care team. Based on these goals and the principle of dignity for all, Caring Across Generations has developed a set of policy recommendations that lay the foundation for the holistic, comprehensive Care Grid of America's future.

SECURE SOCIAL SECURITY

No matter what our political beliefs are, all of us agree that in our golden years we deserve to retire after a lifetime of work and to conclude our lives in dignity and comfort. Most working Americans earn Social Security to provide a basic income for themselves and for their families through their hard work and their Social Security payroll tax contributions. Averaging just $14,000 a year per person, this modest benefit is vitally important to the majority of Americans. According to the AARP, Social Security is "the principal source of income for nearly two-thirds of older American households, and roughly one third of those households depend on Social Security for nearly all of their income."[3] Cuts to Social Security would result in thousands more seniors slipping into poverty.

As it stands now, Social Security has sufficient income and assets to pay 100 percent of benefits for the next two decades and

77 percent of benefits thereafter.[4] One route to that revenue would be to significantly raise the payroll tax cap to $300,000 or $400,000. Currently employers and employees stop paying payroll tax contributions with income over $106,800—this move would affect just the *6 percent* of American workers who earn more than that. There is no reason why millionaires should pay a smaller percentage of payroll taxes than their clerical staff do.

An additional option is broadening the base for Social Security taxes by covering passive income, as policy researchers Virginia Reno and Joni Lavery at the National Academy of Social Insurance argue. Right now, Social Security covers only wages. But it could cover other forms of income such as income from capital, interest on investments, stock dividends, and rental income from real estate, as well as capital gains.[5]

HOME CARE FOR ALL

In the short term, we need to secure and strengthen the existing programs alongside Social Security that provide support to individuals and families, namely, Medicare and Medicaid. Hand in hand with these government supports, we need a refundable tax credit for working-age individuals whose incomes are too high for them to qualify for Medicaid but too low to pay for care. We can't allow the growing group of people in this situation to fall through the cracks. "Of all the forms of inequality," said Dr. Martin Luther King Jr., "injustice in health care is the most shocking and inhumane."[6]

Next, we also can expand upon a model of health care that many experts believe is the gold standard: the Program of All-Inclusive Care for the Elderly (PACE). This is patient-centered, coordinated care. Begun as a pilot program that was funded primarily by foundations, PACE is now a joint program of Medicare and Medicaid operated on the state level; participating states include California, Colorado, Connecticut, Florida, Maine, Michigan, Minnesota, Missouri, New York, Ohio, Vermont, Wisconsin, and the District of Columbia.[7] It is open to people over age fifty-five whose level of need qualifies them for around-the-clock care in a nursing facility; however, the point is to provide enough preventative and ongoing care to keep them out of expensive acute care in nursing homes or hospitals.

If an elderly individual qualifies as sufficiently frail (an average PACE patient has seven different diagnoses), and PACE is available in his or her community, a team of care professionals—physicians, nurses, social workers, physical therapists, home health aides, and others—comes together to assess the elder's medical and care needs, to develop an integrated care plan, and then to provide all the required services. The focus is on a holistic approach developed by this team of not just doctors but all providers, an approach that emphasizes *preventative* services such as frequent checkups, monitoring, and diet and exercise programs, which wind up costing less than diagnostic care. PACE provides medically necessary transportation, some modifications to the home, home care as needed, and recreation, companionship, and meals at PACE Centers. It also provides training and respite for family caregivers and other caregivers.

PACE operates with a fixed annual cost per patient, which is paid by Medicare and Medicaid, depending on the state. It replaces all other health care service providers.

"According to several studies, PACE clients, while far more frail than the average Medicare recipient, cost taxpayers less money in government-funded medical care, have fewer and shorter hospital stays, rarely wind up in nursing homes (even though they must be eligible to enroll in one), and report satisfaction rates close to 100 percent," reported "The New Old Age" column in the *New York Times*. "PACE means care by an interdisciplinary team that knows the patient and family, their histories, strengths, limitations and goals. Team members decide the care plan with each member, tweak it as things change, and rarely say 'no' to anything that will sustain quality of life." [8]

In 2012, there were eighty-eight PACE programs being offered in the previously listed selected states. [9] A program this good at maintaining or even improving quality of life for elders while simultaneously cutting costs should be available everywhere, and for more patients, not just the most frail. Its high start-up costs have stood in the way of further expansion, but we need to bear in mind that when the PACE program is brought to scale, it will generate tens if not hundreds of thousands of new jobs in care management and caregiving while saving money in the long run.

Finally, we must set our sights on a new national program like Social Security that exists specifically to support home- and community-based care in the United States. Regardless of income or assets, every American should be included in this plan, whereby people pay into a fund that they can tap into later in life when they need home care. To support family members who are providing care for their loved ones, the social insurance program should provide them with paid family and medical leave as well as Social Security caregiver credits for those who leave the workforce to provide care. When we account for and support caregiving in this way, we will be making a lasting investment that pays off with benefits for generations to come, as evidenced by the success of the universal social insurance programs in Japan and Germany.

TWENTY-FIRST-CENTURY CARE JOBS

Today, approximately 12 million adults, 40 percent of whom are under the age of sixty-five, are estimated to be in need of long-term care, services, and supports due to disability or functional limitations. Ninety percent of these individuals report receiving unpaid care, while 13 percent of them report using at least some form of paid care. Many of these individuals have unmet care needs because their family caregivers are overburdened, because they cannot afford to hire home care workers, or because government-funded programs provide insufficient coverage for care, services, and supports.

Much of the existing long-term care funded by public programs is based in institutions, nursing homes in particular, yet we know that the great majority—about 90 percent—of Americans want to stay in their homes and stay integrated in their communities for as long as possible. Many studies have proven that people thrive in intergenerational, integrated environments and are able to be productive, full members of their communities for longer.

Home care is the future. That is why it has the fastest-growing workforce in the country. The U.S. Bureau of Labor Statistics expects the workforce to grow by more than 1.6 million direct care workers by 2020. Caring Across Generations estimates that an additional 828,500 home care jobs will be needed over the next decade to meet the needs of the more than 3 million additional individuals who will need care.

Looking at Japan's job growth as a result of their long-term care program, the Geneva Association's Research Programme on Health and Productive Aging notes, "The total number of employees in the LTC service sector has increased from 720,000 in 2000 to almost 1,000,000 in 2004, a 38 percent increase in the period. It is not surprising that most of the increase came from the home-care service sector that has added more than 200,000 employees, with the institutional care sector adding only 70,000 employees." [10]

At a moment when the country is in dire need of solutions to the unemployment crisis, this is a clear solution. The creation of these new jobs could begin now in two steps: increased funding and financing strategies for existing social programs like Medicare and Medicaid that support home care, and rebalancing our social programs to create more support for home- and community-based care as opposed to nursing home care.

IMPROVING JOB QUALITY

Unless we improve the quality of these jobs, the industry will remain unstable, the quality of care will be inconsistent, and we will not be able to retain workers long enough to build their skill level and capacity. With such a large and growing workforce living in poverty, economic inequality will not only persist; it will worsen. We need to improve the quality of home care jobs by raising the wages of both publicly and privately funded home care workers to a minimum of $15 per hour—without cutting into the number of hours of care received by consumers—creating voluntary health and safety standards, and providing paid sick days.

In addition, recognizing that states need to take responsibility for ensuring the availability and accessibility of a well-qualified home care workforce, every state should develop a supportive infrastructure to facilitate consumer-directed programs. This includes taking responsibility for developing quality job conditions and allowing home care workers a voice in policies that impact their lives. States could even make higher wages a condition of participation in state Medicaid programs. Governors could assign their agencies to conduct regular assessments of the home care workforce in their states and provide recommendations on changes to wages to ensure a sufficient number of workers.

BUILDING SKILLS OF CARE

Current federal training requirements for home health aides have not been changed in more than twenty years, and there are no federal standards for training or certification of personal care aides. The fragmented structure of training requirements limits workers' ability to move between long-term care settings and advance along a career path. It also inhibits our ability to develop the workforce we'll need to support a better-coordinated, more efficient system to provide quality long-term care.

Each person's needs are different, every care environment is different, and yet there are certain elements of preparation that can help prevent injury and facilitate a healthy partnership between the care provider and the people receiving supports and services. Training developed in partnership with consumer groups and informed by past efforts to identify core competencies, skills, and knowledge to provide quality care—including the Personal and Home Care Aide State Training Grants; the U.S. Department of Labor Apprenticeship models; and the Center for Medicare and Medicaid Services' Direct Service Workforce Core Competencies road map—offer strong examples.

I've personally witnessed the power of workforce training in my work with nannies. Many of the most committed leaders in Domestic Workers United have gone through the Nanny Training Course. With every cell in their body, domestic workers understand that their work is skilled labor: not every person can do this work and do it well. Providing training validates this truth. It has the potential to lead to improved wages and benefits in a lawless industry. In an environment where workers are constantly feeling invisible and limited, training offers a sense of professionalism along with a concrete pathway to a better future.

CARING CITIZENSHIP

There are at least 11 million people in the United States who are living among us without immigration status. They work, go to school, attend church, start businesses, play on sports teams, and raise families. The United States is home. At least two-thirds of those people are women and children; many of the women are caregivers—for their own families and for others, as paid domestic workers or care providers. There should be a clear road to citizenship for the entire undocumented population. The role that the immigrant workforce will play in helping to address the need for caregiving in the United States is but one of many reasons why we need that road.

We can begin to create the path for undocumented caregivers in the United States by allowing caregivers to adjust their immigration status using work-based criteria in a two-step process. Workers could immediately qualify for a temporary legal status and work authorization based on the demonstration of

employment as a domestic worker or care provider and later receive legal permanent residence based on their continued performance of qualifying employment and completion of training.

We will also need to create channels for workers to migrate
legally to the United States in the future to work as care workers.
Such channels, if they are created, must include portable status,
so workers are not bound by their status to one employer, creating a modern-day slavery-like relationship. Learning from past
guest-worker programs that have undercut wages and hurt the
quality of jobs in an industry, we must ensure that jobs created
through a work-visa program for caregivers are jobs that pay a
living wage with equal worker protections.

And we must address our current immigration enforcement
system. In 2014, we average eleven hundred deportations per day,
not to mention the thousands being held in immigrant detention
centers at any given moment. The people who face deportation
and detention are parents, family members, and workers, including domestic workers. We've learned a lot in recent years about
the human rights crisis that current enforcement policy creates
in immigrant communities, particularly when families are separated. It's time we shifted our priorities away from excessive immigration law enforcement strategies toward an investment in
human potential: integration, education, and workforce development in immigrant communities.

In order for home care to be woven into the fabric of the country,
no one can work in the shadows. Opening a road to citizenship for
the undocumented will help bring the workforce into the full light
of our economy, releasing enormous pressure on workers and
the families who depend on them. No one responsible for caring

for the most precious elements of our lives—our homes and families—should be at risk of being torn from their own homes and families as a result of our immigration policies.

Paying for It

Quality care will cost money. A Care Grid is an investment; however, it also releases a tremendous amount of human resource and potential while creating new efficiencies and cost savings in our health care system. For most people, home care is much less expensive than institution-based care. Many health care experts have begun to study the ways in which enhancing the role of home care providers can help reduce the costs of chronic disease management and significantly reduce the numbers of emergency room visits for older Americans. A 2014 report from the Bipartisan Policy Center called for a bipartisan approach that weaves together financing from publicly funded programs, such as Medicaid, with private insurance products while also improving the efficiency and quality of long-term care.[11]

Our spending reflects our values. Looking at our federal budget today, it's easy to see that defense is a key national priority. I would argue that with the elder boom, we are talking about an urgent matter of national security right at home—the lack of an adequate system to support the millions of older adults who will need care, supports, and services. I believe our national budget should reflect both the importance and the urgency of this investment.

The following are only a few of the many creative ideas that are being explored, where our budget could be shifted to reflect this emerging priority for the nation. And the investment in these jobs will generate new revenue. Many economists have written about the positive impact of higher wages for the lower tiers of the workforce as a result of their spending patterns—they spend at a significantly higher rate than the highest-income earners. That makes improving wages, and expanding this workforce, its own economic stimulus plan.

To bolster Social Security and Medicare, a small increase in the Social Security tax and Medicare tax could ensure the solvency of both programs and increase their benefits. There are many options to fund other programs proposed here. Here are two that haven't been discussed as much: cuts to immigration enforcement as well as incarceration and defense spending and negotiation of lower prices for drugs purchased by Medicare and Medicaid.

IMMIGRATION ENFORCEMENT CUTS

A 2013 report from the Migration Policy Institute calculated the federal government's spending on immigration enforcement in 2012 as more than $17.9 billion. The authors of the report put that amount in perspective: "The US government spends more on its immigration enforcement agencies than on all its other principal criminal federal law enforcement agencies combined. In FY 2012, spending for CBP, ICE, and US-VISIT reached nearly $18 billion. This amount exceeds by approximately 24 percent total spending for the FBI, Drug Enforcement Administration (DEA), Secret Service, U.S. Marshals Service, and Bureau of Alcohol, Tobacco, Firearms, and Explosives (ATF), which stood at $14.4 billion in FY 2012." [12]

NEGOTIATION OF LOWER DRUG PRICES

Currently, the "noninterference" provision in the Medicare Modernization Act expressly prohibits the Medicare program from directly negotiating lower prescription drug prices with pharmaceutical manufacturers. Instead, thousands of private plans compete with one another, trying to attract more customers so they have more leverage to negotiate lower prices with manufacturers. Establishing Medicare and Medicaid as the collective buyer of prescription drugs would harness the purchasing power of millions of beneficiaries of the government programs and would substantially lower prices. Economist Dean Baker calculated that we would have saved $600 billion between 2006 and 2013 if Medicare were allowed to negotiate prices directly with pharmaceutical manufacturers.[13]

Care for a Dance?

A colleague of mine compared the policy change arena to a dance floor. When the first couple is on the dance floor, it's somewhat awkward for others, and for some time, it's just the one couple on the floor. Then one or two bold close friends or family members join the couple. When four or five couples are on the floor, then a critical mass of people feels anonymous enough to get on the floor, and a wave of people get up.

Change occurs in waves—through a combination of the slow and steady work of building model solutions and a powerful movement, and through the bursts of risk and courage that create the space to make leaps forward. With momentum building on the dance floor, we are looking to make our next breakthrough on the national stage.

Clear policy solutions exist. We can shift the federal and state budgets to reflect different priorities. We can create new revenue streams. We can create quality jobs and economic opportunity out of vulnerability. As writer, composer, and philanthropist Peter Buffett said at a forum on the new economy, "These are all just agreements, like the fact that today is Sunday. We can change them."[14] We are resourceful and we are resource rich. When we see a big problem before us, we create big solutions. No solution is ever perfect, because humanity itself is a work in progress, constantly changing and evolving. But we have consistently made progress, one historic step at a time. Now is the time to make history with care.

AFTERWORD

Life in the Care Grid

> We are caught in an inescapable network of mutuality,
> tied into a single garment of destiny. Whatever affects
> one directly affects all indirectly.
>
> —Dr. Martin Luther King Jr.

Not long ago, I heard the mindfulness teacher Sharon Salzberg explain that when she first started learning meditation, she found it remarkably difficult to focus on the breath—to just breathe. It is so easy to get frustrated and impatient; to push too hard, shut down, fall asleep, judge yourself, or want to give up. But her first teacher taught her that what these responses call for is simply being able to return to the breath. "The healing is in the return," she told Sharon.

I believe that the seeds to the future are already deep within us. We already have everything we need to begin. As the world changes and we struggle to find and create solutions in our own lives and in the world around us, we can tap into our legacy. We are part of a long tradition of builders and "solutionaries." We come from a long line of caregivers, stretching back to the beginning of humanity. When we are conscious, we know we have

Miriam has been a vocal leader in efforts to establish rights for care-givers and all domestic workers in California. Now that they have achieved some new protections, she is focused on educating other household workers about the new law. "I love being able to provide el-dercare. That is why I want to improve our jobs. Our work is dignified and we deserve just pay." PHOTOGRAPH BY ALESSANDRA SANGUINETTI the capacity to love: to care for ourselves, for others, and for the whole of the country. We can always return to the basics. And in the return is the healing.

The future will be both reflective of these timeless values and human needs and full of the new—new technology, new modes of communication, new ways of connecting and sharing, new work systems and policies and structures to support it all. We must value and embrace both the new and the old—after all, we are an intergenerational society. This means that we must see and value the threads that are timeless and continue to stay in tune with all that's new and changing.

My friend Sara Horowitz of the Freelancers Union likes to do an exercise where you close your eyes and imagine your ideal community in the future. She has you picture a Monopoly board, but one where you get to decide, block by block, building by building, how you would construct the community. How much green space goes on the board? How many coffee shops and fresh fruit stands? How many playgrounds and schools?

On my board, I focus on the relationships I want to have and allocate space with the intent of nurturing those relationships. I close my eyes and picture the community in which I live when I reach the age of eighty. Here it is:

At eighty, I wake up just before dawn, when the light outside my window is a pale yet soulful blue. I rise slowly and prepare my cup of green tea. While the water is boiling, I get dressed in comfortable clothes for yoga and brush my teeth. I log in to our community message board for our neighborhood apartment complex to let the other yogis know that I'm awake and getting ready to practice. As soon as the clock strikes six, I walk outside to our common space where we practice Ashtanga yoga, a form of yoga traditionally practiced at dawn, and unroll my mat. I am joined by all the other yogis in the community, who greet one another quietly, with sleepy smiles. Our teacher rings the bell, and we sit quietly for two minutes. Then, for forty-five minutes (in my younger days it was an hour and a half), I do a series of Ashtanga yoga postures, skipping the ones that I can no longer do, adjusting the ones that are becoming more difficult, breathing deeply in and out with every pose, the same series I've practiced for fifty years.

I wake into a world of possibility every day. What's possible is both a practical and spiritual matter, and the two are of course connected. There's what's actually possible in the time span of a day, physically, financially, logistically—and then there's our attitude and feelings about what's possible.

For everyone, regardless of who you are, there is much more freedom and choice now that new, expanded government safety nets have been set into place over the last forty years. So now, no matter who you are or what you do, you're eligible for care. Families set up a profile of their care needs, paying an affordable, flat fee for the service, and get matched to someone through an online profile. The rest is covered by our safety net.

I live in an urban community with friends, loved ones, and care providers. I can choose to be in the company of friends and family or to be able to explore things on my own. Much to my own surprise, I have taken up gardening in our community garden and sometimes help with the coordination of volunteers at the garden. We plant Chinese vegetables, including the greens my grandmother used to cook for me. I enjoy cooking with the vegetables and herbs from the garden for the younger people in *our community who don't have as much time to cook, or who come home from school with a healthy appetite.*

If I want to try new things, to take a risk, I have the resources I need. And by resources, I don't just mean money. I mean support to do the things that make me feel alive and help me grow. For me, those things include yoga, art, music of all types, reading biographies, time spent in nature, and intergenerational exchange, particularly time spent with children. I especially enjoy reading with children. As my memory has disappeared, being with children somehow helps me remember. These are the resources that fuel my spirit.

Between caregivers, friends, and family, I have a web of support to help me live life fully even as activities of daily living get harder and as my body and energy change. I can count on care providers every day. They have helped me recover from my last injury, a broken leg from a fall during the winter. They and their families live in the same community. Our community has child care set up for everyone. Caregivers work reasonable hours, for fair wages, with plenty of time off to spend with their own families to explore and experience the world as they choose.

In the afternoon, my caregiver picks up her children from school and brings them over. We make a snack together—my favorite is apples with peanut butter and raisins—and then I help them with their homework, except for math, which was never my best subject. Afterward we play one another music we like, introducing each other to oldies from the early 2000s alongside all the hot new groups.

One evening per week, I host happy hour in my home, where an intergenerational gathering of friends, family, and community—including all of our caregivers and their families—comes together to share food and drink and have lively debates about politics, popular culture, and the future. Everyone brings something—we challenge ourselves to create, find, and share new recipes. Those who don't cook have to bring a new question for the group to discuss or a new game for the group to play. We encourage the sharing of skills and wisdom. Believing that wisdom comes of every action, reaction, and mistake, we have developed a culture of support, doing our best to understand and be good to one another despite generational and other differences and the human tendency toward gossip.

Everyone of every age is oriented toward living the fullest life possible and the choice to define what that means for ourselves. Just the way roads make it possible for us to choose which direction to go, so this new, universal care system, the Care Grid, makes this freedom possible. At the heart of it all are relationships. They are key to feeling we have the resources and freedom to seize upon the possibilities before us. At eighty, I aim to end each day knowing I lived to the fullest extent possible.

I turned forty on February 5, 2014. It was a milestone year, and I wasn't afraid of it. This felt significant to me. When I stopped to think about the moment in my life, I noted some important, encouraging truths. I have a good amount of experience and practice at a good number of things. I have relationships that have lasted a long time—decades, in some cases. I have a really grounded sense that every day is a series of choices that are in my hands to make. And I even have a sense of which of those choices might be better than others. I know when I'm taking a risk. And I generally know what risk is worth taking, or I know whom I trust to ask for advice on the question. I know that there's not much that's unique to me—I'll probably find that someone else is struggling with a similar pain point or question. It's not that everything's certain or clear—in fact, it's quite clear at this point that nothing is certain—but I have a certain foundation to navigate through the twists and turns that life brings.

As a nation addressing the unfolding care crisis, there are some similar dynamics. There will always be unknowns, but there's a lot that we do know. There's a wealth of collective experience and knowledge. We know, for example, that people prefer to live in their own homes until the end, where they have a better quality of life and death. We know that training can help prepare both professional and unpaid caregivers to provide effective support. And we know that there are things we need to do as individuals to prepare for what's to come, alongside things we can count on family, community, service providers, and the government to do for us.

We have a tremendous number of resources to help us make good choices—from models of government support in other countries, to health care models we've tried at home and can scale; from time-honored practices like trading time spent caregiving with one another to give each other respite, to new technologies that make this kind of trading of services easier; from ancient philosophical and spiritual teachings about death to modern advances in Western medicine that relieve pain.

In the United States, we need to reorient the goals and purpose of our systems. Ideally, we would be shifting the way we treat our stages of life so that each and every person can trust that when the end of life comes, whenever it comes, they will have had the support and resources to have lived fully to the very end. There's no changing the fear and pain of the loss of life. However, we can change what the experience of life is before we die. If we could create enough of a universal baseline of support, such that each and every person in this nation could choose to live life fully, on their terms for as long as possible, it would transform our ability as a nation to thrive economically, politically, culturally, and spiritually.

To me, this means establishing a universal baseline of care and support for everyone, regardless of age, ability, occupation, or employment; a system to bring care to every home and community. And it means a revaluing of care as a fundamental and necessary resource, embedded in our ability to live free as people. We must therefore embed it in our national infrastructure and make care visible and universal. In so doing, we could create millions of good jobs caring and supporting one another, jobs that you can truly take pride in and that pay a wage that can support your family. I think about the Care Grid as a matter of national security. Caregivers offer peace, freedom, and security for millions of Americans.

The Care Grid is the answer to the elder boom. Not only will it support the transformation we're all going through together; it will release the unstoppable power of that transformation to improve our lives and secure our future.

ACKNOWLEDGMENTS

This book and the body of work that it emerges from are a manifestation of the labor of love on the part of many, many people. In particular I would like to thank:

Ariane Conrad, the one and only book doula—true, deep gratitude for your partnership and hard work bringing this book into being.

Sarita Gupta and Mariana Viturro, for your leadership and for taking big leaps of faith with me, year after year. And Felicia Martinez and Irene Jor for everything you do to support me.

The staff (past and present), partners, and supporters of Caring Across Generations, for your faith, creativity, and commitment to our shared vision for a caring America.

The staff, members, and supporters of the National Domestic Workers Alliance, for all the love with which you're building our movement.

The staff and members of Hand in Hand: The Domestic Employers Network, for your practice of interdependence.

Michele Asselin, Alessandra Sanguinetti, and the Magnum Foundation, for the beautiful imagery in this book.

All the people whose stories make this book come alive, including my grandfathers, Mrs. Sun, my grandmother, my mom, my aunt, Michael Levine, Robin Shaffert, Marlene Champion, Nicie Hassell, Erlinda Alferez, Diki, Eliza Morales, Diony Verdaguer, Becky Tarbotton, Nikki Brown-Booker, Marjorie Dove Kent, and Victor Quintana.

Van Jones, Lezlie Frye, Linda Burnham, Alicia Garza, Andrea Cristina Mercado, Ryan Senser, Jee Kim, Bridgit Evans, Simon Greer, Lee Goldberg, Suzanne Wall, Harmony Goldberg, Elizabeth Lesser, and Marc Favreau and Jed Bickman at The New Press, all of whose feedback and suggestions were invaluable.

The Prime Movers Fellowship, for enabling me to imagine writing a book.

Tony Lu, for thirteen years of patient, unconditional support.

My family, for everything—especially their patience with me spending our vacations working on this book.

George and Adelaide Goehl, for the caring home we're creating together.

APPENDIX A

Government Programs Related to Aging and Care

Social Security

Social Security provides basic financial support to retired people, generally those over the age of sixty-five to sixty-seven. Having paid into the fund for at least ten years (technically, forty quarters; in other words, the ten years do not have to be continuous) over the course of their working lives (together with their employers), senior citizens can, theoretically, rely on the accumulated funds once they are no longer able or willing to work. According to the Social Security Administration, the average monthly Social Security benefit for a retired worker was about $1,230 (or $14,760 per year) at the beginning of 2012. The AARP says that Social Security is "the principal source of income for nearly two-thirds of older American households, and roughly one third of those households depend on Social Security for nearly all of their income."[1] Many women and people of color, who on average earn less income during their working years, face particular struggles to make ends meet during retirement.

While the future of Social Security, our fundamental social insurance program, is solid, it needs ongoing fine-tuning as our demographics change. For one thing, it relies on the employment of younger workers, who pay in what gets paid out to retirees. When Social Security was created in the 1930s, about 5 percent of the population was sixty-five or older. Now more than 13 percent of Americans are over sixty-five, and by 2030, 20 percent will be. Although our workforce is vastly more productive, this still leaves a gap in financing. Although the Social Security trust fund has a surplus, built up intentionally to cover the increase in the number of beneficiaries over the last two decades, that surplus will be depleted by 2033 and current revenues will cover only 77 percent of benefits.

Supplemental Security Income, Housing Assistance, and Food Stamps

Elders with very low or no incomes—often the oldest of the old (which could happen to most of us even if we've been able to save a fair sum)—are eligible to receive several types of government assistance. In 1974 the Nixon administration created Supplemental Security Income, a federal assistance program to replace state-based programs for low-income individuals with disabilities and elderly individuals. The program radically reduced the number of elders then living in poverty. Today more than 2 million elders receive Supplemental Security Income benefits: a monthly check of up to $698 for an individual and $1,048 for a couple (in 2012) to help meet the costs of basic needs such as food, shelter, and clothing.

Supplemental Security Income recipients are also automatically entitled to Section 8, or assistance with rent in public housing projects, rentals from landlords who accept the vouchers, or housing built specifically for the elderly under the Section 202 program. Some of these housing situations include funding for a service coordinator, who arranges transportation, meal services, housekeeping, medication management, haircuts, and social activities, as well as visits from nurses, dentists, and therapists.

Elders who need assistance with three or more activities for daily life used to be eligible to receive assistance under the Congregate Housing Services Program, which provides meals, housekeeping, personal care, and transportation; the program stopped receiving funding in 1995, although those in the program before that date continue to receive support. In 2000, the Assisted Living Conversion Program was created to allow HUD-subsidized facilities for elderly residents to modify their living space to accommodate their specific needs. All of these special housing programs were designed to keep elders from having to move into nursing homes and instead allow them to remain in their homes and communities, which translates into major cost savings. Nevertheless, each budgeting round has placed these programs at risk of severe cuts.

Low-income elders can also benefit from the food stamps program (now formally called the Supplemental Nutrition Assistance Program), another federal assistance program, although according to the Food Research and Action Center (FRAC), only one-third of seniors who are eligible actually participate in the program. FRAC believes this is partially because of the stigma and partially because of a lack of information or awareness about eligibility.

Medicare

Medicare is the basic health care program for those over the age of sixty-five and people with disabilities. Like Social Security, the program is funded in part by employees' and employers' taxes. Unlike the payments you receive from Social Security, the amount you receive from Medicare is linked to your medical needs, not how much income you earned in your lifetime. On average, Medicare covers about half the medical costs of those who enroll, although there are no caps on out-of-pocket costs and many seniors with very high medical costs face significant financial difficulties.[2] According to the U.S. Department of Health and Human Services, the number of people enrolled in Medicare more than doubled between 1966 and 2002, from less than 20 million to more than 40 million, due to population growth, population aging, and added coverage for those with disabilities, end-stage renal failure, and ALS. In 2012, more than 49 million Americans were enrolled.

Medicare is organized into four basic parts: A, B, C, and D. Medicare Part A covers inpatient hospitalization, skilled nursing care, and hospice.[3] Part B covers visits to doctors and testing in a traditional fee-for-service model; you pay a monthly premium (adjusted annually; in 2014, most people paid a premium of $104 per month) and a deductible of $147 per year, after which 80 percent of approved costs are covered. To cover those remaining costs, you can opt to buy a Medicare supplement plan from a private insurer. Medicare Part C, also known as the Medicare Advantage Plan, is the managed care version of Medicare that covers the benefits mentioned previously, plus prescription drugs. Part C offers patients lower costs and often extra benefits, but patients can select only from within the network of doctors and hospitals. Part D enables outpatient prescription drug coverage in conjunction with either the Medicare Advantage Plan (Part C) or a private prescription drug plan.

Unfortunately, many of elders' health-related needs are not addressed by Medicare coverage. The progressive chronic conditions common to those over the age of eighty often don't get resolved with the surgery, hospitalization, or new technologies that Medicare covers: they simply require ongoing support and care going forward. Yet long-term care is mostly uncovered, whether it is needed at home or in a facility. As the helpful booklet from Medicare informs us: "Medicare doesn't cover custodial care if it is the only kind of care you need. Custodial care is care that helps you with usual daily activities like getting in and out of bed, eating, bathing, dressing, and using the bathroom. It may also include care that most people do themselves, like using eye drops, oxygen, and taking care of colostomy or bladder catheters." [4] Only for strictly medical support as they define it, such as administering intravenous injections or providing physical therapy mandated by a physician, will a certain number of hours of skilled nursing care be covered. Hospitalization in an acute-care facility for at least three days enables a Medicare-sponsored stay of up to one hundred days in a skilled nursing facility. [5] Other kinds of living arrangements such as assisted living may be suitable for someone with long-term care needs but are not covered by Medicare.

Doctors' visits are covered, but in many communities it is difficult to find a doctor who is taking new Medicare patients. In

Chapter 1 I mentioned the drastically insufficient number of geriatricians in the United States. The reason for this shortage is discussed there as well: geriatrics is unpopular because it isn't as profitable as other specialties. Medicare reimbursements are modeled on standard procedures, with an emphasis on specialists and expensive technologies. Medicare's fee-for-service payment model encourages billable services but not the continuity of care that elders mostly need.

Medicaid

Medicaid is a means-tested program that covers a wide range of medical and long-term care services to individuals who have sufficiently low income. Under the Affordable Care Act, many states have expanded Medicaid to provide coverage for acute care needs for anyone with income under 138 percent of the federal poverty line. For states that have not expanded Medicaid under the Affordable Care Act, and even in so-called expansion states, Medicaid covers long-term care for certain categories of people: seniors with low enough income and few enough assets to be eligible for Supplemental Security Income, some people with disabilities, and certain categories of women and children and seniors with medical bills sufficiently high to leave them with very low income and very few assets. Funded by a combination of federal and state sources, Medicaid is managed at the local level, and different states have different eligibility requirements and benefits; some states, for example, have very few home- and community-based services. Applications are long and rigorous, requiring copies of all kinds of certificates and policies that even the most organized among us would be hard-pressed to pull together, although institutional providers like hospitals and nursing homes are quite adept at qualifying people. Eldercare lawyers, on the other hand, charge thousands of dollars to handle them, as much as $10,000 in places such as New York City.

Medicaid is the largest source of funding for nursing home stays. More than 40 percent of the costs of America's nursing home care was paid by Medicaid in 2008. States have the option to add home- and community-based services like personal care services (home care), but some provide it to all beneficiaries with a functional need and some have a limited number of slots (other applicants may be put on a waiting list). Approximately two-thirds of states offer personal care services to all beneficiaries who demonstrate a need that meets the eligibility requirement, while the remaining states have a program that provides home- and community-based care to certain geographic areas. Depending on the state, Medicaid sometimes pays for family members to provide care at home or in the community. This covers an important gap in services not funded by Medicare.

Medicaid is different from Medicare, which is a social insurance program that working people contribute to via payroll taxes; Medicaid is a social safety net or social welfare program that helps certain vulnerable populations. In the United States, however, there is a stigma attached to social welfare programs; people who enroll in the programs are often assigned the demeaning label "charity case." Yet increasingly, seniors who spent their lives in the middle class, even the upper-middle class, are living so long that they simply run out of money and must rely on the program.

Older Americans Act

In 1965, the Older Americans Act (OAA) was passed as part of Lyndon Johnson's Great Society reforms. It established the federal Administration on Aging, to coordinate comprehensive services with a network of state and local agencies on aging. This is the kind of large-scale, cross-sector initiative we need to coordinate efforts and to support Americans of all backgrounds as they age. OAA-funded programs are not means-tested and are open to all individuals over the age of sixty.

OAA services include home- and community-based support, wellness and disease-prevention programs, protection of elder rights, and the National Family Caregiver Support Program. Although there are no specific financial eligibility criteria for OAA services, they are intended primarily for low-income, frail seniors over age sixty and seniors living in rural areas. Specific funds exist for Native American elders. Unfortunately, the program's funding has never been adequate to meet its goals.

In 2010, the most recent year for which service data are available, OAA provided for more than 35 million hours of personal care, homemaker, and chore services—assistance with activities such as eating, dressing, bathing, shopping, or light housework. More than seven hundred thousand caregivers took advantage of services like counseling, training, and respite care (6.8 million hours provided) through the National Family Caregiver Program. (Some family caregivers also benefited from the Family and Medical Leave Act, which is geared toward a broader population and mandates some employers to permit unpaid leave for those caring for family members; however, as I described in Chapter 2, most family caregivers cannot or do not take this option.) And despite the obvious usefulness of a solution that involves paid caregivers, none of these programs support such initiatives as training, formalization of hiring conditions, and improved attitudes toward paid caregivers.

APPENDIX B

Resources for Families

For Conversations Between Family Members and Elders

Here are some ideas for ways to set the stage for positive, productive, and respectful family dialogues, which ideally should be regular, low-pressure family events, instead of being framed as "the Conversation," a high-stakes, high-pressure event when a crisis is looming or already under way, similar to "the Talk" that often accompanies approaching puberty in childhood. If a family conversation does take place during or after a crisis moment, such as an elder's sudden fall and hospitalization, it is better to address issues one at a time rather than trying to tackle everything at once.

- The setting should be comfortable and the time frame open-ended, so everyone feels relaxed and able to focus and participate.
- If there is discomfort or resistance to talking about delicate issues such as diminishing health, the need for professional support, estate planning, or death, first talking about the situation of a friend or relative may provide an opening.

Guidance from someone outside the family who everyone respects might also help.

- Have someone take notes, especially if topics such as advanced health care directives (living wills) or financial planning need to be resolved.
- Ask elders where they keep important documents such as insurance policies, wills, financial records, health records, and the like. If documents are missing, make a plan to find or create them.
- Make plans to research the options for housing, home care, health care, care managers, and so on, and divide the tasks among family members. Everyone should feel included and responsible, particularly elders. Plan another meeting to review the options, and create a lot of room for elders to express their preferences.

For Families Hiring a Professional Caregiver

Most employers of professional caregivers want to do the right thing, but it isn't always clear what "the right thing" means. Having universal guidelines and minimum standards is beneficial for both employer and employee. Guidelines and standards provide a baseline from which employer and employee can negotiate. A responsible employer has a conversation with a worker about wages, expectations, and hours, pays the worker on time, pays the worker a living wage—generally around $15 per hour—and offers benefits such as paid days off, paid holidays, and sick days. Ultimately it's in employers' own interests to give employees time off: workers stay rested and healthy, which means they are able to be present and attentive in the home—and if they are caring for a child or parent, employers want them to be at their best. As it stands now, caregivers burn out fast because of low wages and poor working conditions.

The Hand-in-Hand Domestic Employers Network has developed the following resources for employers seeking support in how to create healthy and fair employment relationships:

FAIRCARE PLEDGE

I affirm the value of all care work in our community and believe fair employment practices help create mutually beneficial relationships between employers and domestic workers—nannies/child care providers, housecleaners, and home attendants for seniors or people with disabilities. When I employ someone in my home, I pledge to be a respectful and fair employer, recognizing that my home is someone's workplace. (domesticemployers.org /get-involved/)

EMPLOYER CHECKLIST

Here's a set of best practices to support caring homes and fair workplaces:

- Develop a mutually negotiated work agreement
- Create opportunities for open and clear communication to build trust and address concerns
- Pay a living wage of at least $15/hour

- Provide paid time off for illness, medical appointments, vacations, and holidays
- Provide notice and severance pay when the working relationship comes to an end
- Comply with existing basic protections for workers, such as Domestic Workers' Bills of Rights
- Advocate for policies that create fair jobs and make child care and in-home support affordable

For more information about the Hand-in-Hand Domestic Employers Network and its resources for families hiring professional caregivers, you can consult the organization's website (domestic employers.org), Facebook page (www.facebook.com/domestic employers), and Twitter feed (twitter.com/HiHemployers).

JOIN—OR CREATE YOUR OWN VERSION OF—ELDERCARE DIALOGUES

Sample themes and topics for dialogues, with the ultimate goal of transforming caring relationships in our society, include:

- Shared vision for caring and interdependent communities
- Story circles including elder caregivers, seniors, family caregivers
- Intergenerational storytelling about changes in culture, work, and politics.
- The relationships between care, gender, and migration
- The care economy—understanding the role that care plays in our economy
- Disability rights and understanding ableism

See the website for Jews for Racial and Economic Justice (www.jfrej.org) for more details.

For Employers of Unpaid Family Caregivers

Flexible hours, paid sick time, and paid family leave have been shown to enhance employee productivity, lower absenteeism, reduce costs, and therefore increase profits. Employers can also educate and train their supervisors and managers on how to be sensitive to the needs of caregiving employees. They can offer support groups, referrals to community-based caregiver resources, and discounted backup home care for emergencies. As payers of health care benefits, many employers are also in a position to influence health care providers to better support family caregivers' needs for information and training. Exerting this influence could go a long way in helping caregivers stay on the job as productive and valued employees.

To help support these kinds of practices, a coalition of employers called ReACT (Respect a Caregiver's Time) was founded in 2010. ReACT is composed of corporations and organizations dedicated to creating work environments where the challenges faced by caregivers juggling the demands of both work and caregiving for an adult with a chronic age-related disease are understood and recognized. They provide support and resources that employees need to meet and balance their personal responsibilities for caregiving and their professional demands. See ReACT's website (respectcaregivers.org) for more information.

Resources Related to Health Care and Home Care for Elders

THE PRIMARY DOCTOR

Do everything in your power to maintain an existing, long-standing relationship between a general practitioner or internist and your aging relative. If the elder has to move and leave behind his or her doctor (or if the practice closes or the practitioner relocates), make sure to get a personal referral from the old doctor before the move, which may make it easier to be accepted in a new practice—many won't accept elders or will make it very challenging to get an appointment. Make sure the elder's medical records are clear and well organized, not reams of illegible handwriting from multiple doctors. Choose one family member to be the point person for all questions and information: this same person should accompany the elder on every doctor's visit, as much as possible.

HOME MODIFICATIONS

The Department of Health and Human Services, Administration on Aging, has created a checklist of things to consider when renovating a home, to make it more accessible later in life:[1]

APPLIANCES, KITCHEN, BATHROOM
- Are cabinet doorknobs easy to use?
- Are stove controls easy to use and clearly marked?
- Are faucets easy to use?

- Are there grab bars where needed?
- Are all appliances and utensils conveniently and safely located?
- Can the oven and refrigerator be opened easily?
- Can you sit down while working?
- Can you get into and out of the bathtub or shower easily?
- Is the kitchen counter height and depth comfortable for you?
- Is the water temperature regulated to prevent scalding or burning?
- Would you benefit from having convenience items, such as a handheld showerhead, a garbage disposal, or a trash compactor?

CLOSETS, STORAGE SPACES
- Are your closets and storage areas conveniently located?
- Are your closet shelves too high?
- Can you reach items in the closet easily?
- Do you have enough storage space?
- Have you gotten the maximum use out of the storage space you have, including saving space with special closet shelf systems and other products?

DOORS, WINDOWS
- Are your doors and windows easy to open and close?
- Are your door locks sturdy and easy to operate?
- Are your doors wide enough to accommodate a walker or wheelchair?
- Do your doors have peepholes or viewing?

DRIVEWAY, GARAGE

- Does your garage door have an automatic opener?
- Is your parking space always available?
- Is your parking space close to the entrance of your home?

ELECTRICAL OUTLETS, SWITCHES, SAFETY DEVICES

- Are light or power switches easy to turn on and off?
- Are electrical outlets easy to reach?
- Are the electrical outlets properly grounded to prevent shocks?
- Are your extension cords in good condition?
- Can you hear the doorbell in every part of the house?
- Do you have smoke detectors throughout your home?
- Do you have an alarm system?
- Is the telephone readily available for emergencies?
- Would you benefit from having an assistive device to make it easier to hear and talk on the telephone?

FLOORS

- Are all of the floors in your home on the same level?
- Are steps up and down marked in some way?
- Are all floor surfaces safe and covered with nonslip or non-skid materials?
- Do you have scatter rugs or doormats that could be hazardous?

HALLWAYS, STEPS, STAIRWAYS

- Are hallways and stairs in good condition?
- Do all of your hallways and stairs have smooth, safe surfaces?

- Do your stairs have steps that are big enough for your whole foot?
- Do you have handrails on both sides of the stairway?
- Are your stair rails wide enough for you to grasp them securely?
- Would you benefit from building a ramp to replace the stairs or steps inside or outside of your home?

LIGHTING, VENTILATION

- Do you have night-lights where they are needed?
- Is the lighting in each room sufficient for the use of the room?
- Is the lighting bright enough to ensure safety?
- Is each room well-ventilated with good air circulation?

The National Resource Center on Supportive Housing and Home Modifications is a clearinghouse for news on government-assisted housing, assisted-living policies, and home modifications for elders. Visit the center's home modifications website (www.homemods.org) for more information.

Resources in Preparing for Death

LIVING WILL VERSUS HEALTH CARE PROXY

A living will specifies the treatments an individual wants in case of a near-death situation. Living wills are not acknowledged in every state, and even where they are, a doctor may choose not to follow them because he or she fears a lawsuit from the family or because of the doctor's personal beliefs. The durable power of attorney for health care appoints another person, usually a family member, to make health care decisions. That person is known as the health care proxy. Jane Gross writes:

> The standard language in a living will means one thing at fifty and another thing at ninety. Your definition of quality of life can change to encompass previously unthinkable things, like paralysis. No living will can account for that, can itemize all contingencies across the great arc of time and circumstance, unless its writer were to do little else but update the document. It is the proxy's job to understand this, to grasp both the abiding principles of what a loved one would want and the ever-changing details and attitudes. A well-chosen health care proxy appreciates that the line will move and decisions must intuitively move with it.[2]

FIVE WISHES FOR AGING WITH DIGNITY

Five Wishes combines a living will and health care power of attorney and applies in forty-two of fifty states. It is available in many languages. Five Wishes was introduced in 1997 and originally distributed with support from a grant by the Robert Wood Johnson Foundation.

Five Wishes lets your family and doctors know:

- Who you want to make health care decisions for you when you can't make them.
- The kind of medical treatment you want or don't want.

- How comfortable you want to be.
- How you want people to treat you.
- What you want your loved ones to know.[3]

Find out more about Five Wishes at the Aging with Dignity website (www.agingwithdignity.org/five-wishes.php).

APPENDIX C

Ways to Get Involved

Caring Across Generations

Caring Across Generations is a national movement inspiring people to value connections across generations, promoting policies protecting the dignity and independence of seniors, people with disabilities, and people who support and care for them.

To learn more, visit: www.caringacross.org

Facebook: www.facebook.com/caringacrossgenerations

Twitter: twitter.com/CaringAcrossGen

Family Values @ Work

Family Values @ Work is a national network of twenty-one state and local coalitions helping spur the growing movement for family-friendly workplace policies such as paid sick days and paid family leave. Too many people have to risk their jobs to care for a loved one or have to put a family member at risk to keep a job. We're made to feel that this is a personal problem, but it's political—family values too often end at the workplace door. We need new workplace standards to meet the needs of real families today.

To get involved, visit: familyvaluesatwork.org

Facebook: www.facebook.com/FamilyValuesAtWork?fref=ts

Twitter: twitter.com/FmlyValuesWork

My Home Is Someone's Workplace

My Home Is Someone's Workplace calls on employers to recognize that their homes are workplaces and take the Fair Care Pledge to commit to fair and respectful employment practices that benefit both workers and employers. Most people want to do the right thing for their families and for the workers they employ in their homes—but it isn't always clear what doing the right thing means. That's why the Fair Care Pledge comes with a Checklist that supports employers by providing guidelines and best practices they can follow. My Home Is Someone's Workplace also brings the conversation about the domestic workplace out from behind closed doors and into our communities, building cultural recognition of the value of domestic labor. It is a project of Hand-in-Hand: The Domestic Employers Network, a network of employers of nannies, housecleaners, and home attendants, our families and allies, who believe that dignified and respectful working conditions benefit employer and workers alike.

To learn more, visit: domesticemployers.org

Facebook: www.facebook.com/domesticemployers

Twitter: twitter.com/HiHemployers

The Aging Mastery Program ™

The Aging Mastery Program (AMP) is a behavior change incentive program for aging well. AMP combines goal-setting and peer support to help individuals develop positive habits across many dimensions that lead to improved health, stronger financial security, and overall well-being. The program is interactive by design, presenting participants with a variety of opportunities to take part in activities that reinforce behavior change and also earn rewards. AMP is distributed and supported by the National Council on Aging (NCOA), along with a nationwide network of nonprofit partners.

To learn more, visit: www.ncoa.org/amp

Domestic Workers' Bill of Rights

Despite the important work they do, domestic workers have been left out of many basic labor protections afforded to other workers. The National Domestic Workers Alliance and its member organizations are working to right this historic wrong through their Domestic Workers' Bill of Rights campaigns. These campaigns have combined the effort to eliminate the exclusion of domestic workers from state labor and employment laws with attempts to raise standards through more expansive legislative protections.

To learn more, visit: www.domesticworkers.org/initiatives/labor-protections

Facebook: www.facebook.com/nationaldomesticworkersalliance

Twitter: twitter.com/domesticworkers

Make It Work

Make It Work is a community of women and men coming together to share their experiences and seek better solutions so that everyone is paid fairly for her or his work and hardworking Americans don't need to choose between being there for family and earning a living. This means promoting equal pay for equal work, a higher minimum wage, paid family and sick leave, and affordable childcare and eldercare. After all, people who work hard deserve to make more than a decent living—we deserve to have a decent life.

To join the conversation, visit: www.makeitworkcampaign.org

Facebook: www.facebook.com/miwcampaign

Twitter: twitter.com/MIWCampaign

We Belong Together: Women for Common Sense Immigration Reform

Immigration reform is rarely thought of as a women's issue, but in fact it is central to the fight for women's equality. Millions of immigrant women who are part of the fabric of our communities, workplaces, and schools are blocked from achieving their full potential because of a broken immigration system. We Belong Together is an initiative of the National Domestic Workers Alliance, the National Asian Pacific American Women's Forum, and dozens of other women's organizations to bring forward the voices and experiences of women to help shape the future of immigration policy.

To join, visit: www.webelongtogether.org
Facebook: www.facebook.com/pages/We-Belong-Together
/207549645977714
Twitter: twitter.com/WomenBelong

Center for Community Change Action: Grassroots Voices for Retirement Security Campaign

The Center for Community Change Action is a national organization that works to strengthen, connect, and mobilize grassroots groups to enhance their leadership, voice, and power. In 2011 the Center for Community Change Action brought grassroots organizations together to work on protecting and improving Social Security, Medicare, and Medicaid. Since then, they have organized hundreds of events, published dozen of op-eds, met with and moved dozens of members of Congress, educated thousands of people, collected dozens of stories, and led numerous get-out-the-vote activities. In 2013 they launched the Grassroots Ambassador program to more effectively recruit, train, and engage leaders in their local communities.

For more information, visit: www.retirementsecurityvoices .org

The Future of Work

The Future of Work is a national movement challenging the persistent insecurity experienced by millions of American workers, stemming from increasingly contingent and precarious employment. Anchored by the National Guestworkers Alliance, Jobs with Justice, and National People's Action, the Future of Work movement organizes working families across industries to help us reimagine the role of government in protecting workers, including lifting up the basic right to full and fair employment.

For more information, visit: www.guestworkeralliance.org

Jobs with Justice's Future of Work website: www.jwj.org /our-work/issues/shaping-the-future-of-work

National People's Action Future of Work website: npa-us .org/futureofwork

NOTES

Introduction: Caring Across Generations

1. Bureau of Labor Statistics, U.S. Department of Labor, Occupational Outlook Handbook, 2010–11, Home Health Aides and Personal and Home Care Aides, www.bls.gov/ooh/healthcare/personal-care-aides.htm.

2. Paraprofessional Healthcare Institute, "Occupational Projections for Direct_Care Workers, 2008–2018," *PHI Facts* 1 (February 2010), directcare clearinghouse.org/download/PHI%20FactSheet1Update_singles%20(2).pdf.

1. The Elder Boom

1. Thomas Kirkwood, "Why Women Live Longer," *Scientific American*, October 1, 2010, www.scientificamerican.com/article.cfm?id=why-women -live-longer.

2. National Aging Information Center, U.S. Administration on Aging, *Aging in the Twenty-First Century* (Washington, DC: Government Printing Office, 1996).

3. Robert Butler, Nancy Etcoff, Susie Orbach, and Heidi D'Agostino, "Beauty Comes of Age," study commissioned by Dove Soap, September 2006, www.anneofcarversville.com/storage/research-dove-study/Beauty% 20Comes%20of%20Age%202006%20Dove%20Global%20Study%20on%20 Aging%20Beauty%20and%20Well-being.pdf.

4. Nicole S. Dahmen and Raluca Cozma, eds., *Media Takes: On Aging* (New York: International Longevity Center; Sacramento: Aging Services of California, 2009).

5. Jared Diamond, "How Societies Can Grow Old Better," TED Talks, November 2013, www.ted.com/talks/jared_diamond_how_societies_can _grow_old_better/transcript#t-984616.

6. M. Sidell, J. Katz, and C. Komaromy, *Death and Dying in Residential and Nursing Homes for Older People: Examining the Case for Palliative Care*, report for the Department of Health (Milton Keynes, UK: Open University, 1997).

7. Jeanine Skowronski, "Cost of Long-Term Care Rises," *Daily Beast*, October 29, 2010, www.newsweek.com/cost-long-term-care-rises-74109.

8. "Nursing Homes: Cost and Coverage," AARP.org, assets.aarp.org /external_sites/caregiving/options/nursing_home_costs.html.

9. "National Spending for Long-Term Services and Supports (LTSS), 2011," National Health Policy Forum of the George Washington University, February 1, 2013.

10. Nari Rhee and Diane Oakley, *The Retirement Savings Crisis: Is It Worse Than We Think?* (Washington, DC: National Institute on Retirement Security, 2013).

11. AARP, "AARP to Congress and the President: Don't Cut Social Security," press release, December 18, 2012, www.aarp.org/about-aarp/press -center/info-12-2012/AARP-to-Congress-and-the-President-Dont-Cut -Social-Security.html.

12. LongTermCare.gov, "Costs of Care," longtermcare.gov/costs-how -to-pay/costs-of-care/.

13. Ibid.; LongTermCare.gov, "Costs and How to Pay," www.long termcare.gov/LTC/Main_Site/Paying/Index.aspx.

14. *Alzheimer's Disease and Dementia*, report of the Special Committee on Aging, U.S. Senate, December 2012, www.gpo.gov/fdsys/pkg/CRPT-112 srpt254/pdf/CRPT-112srpt254.pdf.

15. Stephen P. Juraschek, Xiaoming Zhang, Vinoth K. Ranganathan, and Vernon Lin, "United States Registered Nurse Workforce Report Card and Shortage Forecast," *Public Health Resources* paper 149 (2012).

16. Bruce Brittain, "Many Geriatrics, Few Geriatricians," Changing Aging, February 27, 2013, changingaging.org/blog/many-geriatrics-few -geriatricians/.

17. Joanne Lynn, *Sick to Death and Not Going to Take It Anymore!* (Berkeley: University of California Press, 2004).

18. Ibid.

19. Lynn, *Sick to Death*, 11.

2. The Sandwich Generation

1. Gail Sheehy, *Passages in Caregiving* (New York: William Morrow, 2010), p. 20.

2. National Alliance for Caregiving and AARP, *Caregiving in the United States*, funded by MetLife Foundation, is a trio of comparative studies conducted in 1997, 2004, and 2009. Statistics reflect the latest survey, from 2009.

3. Celia Watson Seupel, "The Job to End All Others," *New York Times*, June 13, 2011, newoldage.blogs.nytimes.com/2011/06/13/the-job-to-end-all -others/.

4. Sandra Tsing-Loh, "Daddy Issues," *The Atlantic*, February 6, 2012, www.theatlantic.com/magazine/archive/2012/03/daddy-issues/308890 /?single_page=true.

5. AARP Florida, "The Sandwich Generation: You Are Not Alone," June 28, 2012, www.aarp.org/home-family/caregiving/info-06-2012/sand wich-generation-fl1845.html.

6. National Alliance for Caregiving and AARP, *Caregiving in the United States 2009*.

7. Charles R. Pierret, "The 'Sandwich Generation': Women Caring for Parents and Children," *Monthly Labor Review*, September 2006.

8. *Alzheimer's Disease and Dementia*, report of the Special Committee on Aging, U.S. Senate, December 2012, www.gpo.gov/fdsys/pkg/CRPT -112srpt254/pdf/CRPT-112srpt254.pdf.

9. Joanne Lynn, *Sick to Death and Not Going to Take It Anymore!* (Berkeley: University of California Press, 2004).

10. R. Schulz and S. Beach, "Caregiving as a Risk Factor for Mortality: The Caregiver Health Effects Study," *Journal of the American Medical Association* 282, no. 23 (1999): 2215–19; R. Schulz, P. Visintainer, and G.M. Williamson, "Psychiatric and Physical Morbidity Effect of Caregiving," *Journal of Gerontology* 45, no. 5 (1990): 181–91.

11. Linda Barrett, *Caregivers: Life Changes and Coping Strategies* (Washington, DC: AARP Public Policy Institute, 2013), www.aarp.org/content/dam/aarp/research/surveys_statistics/general/2013/Caregivers-Life-Changes-and-Coping-Strategies-AARP-rsa-gen.pdf.

12. National Alliance for Caregiving and AARP, *Caregiving in the United States 2009.*

13. Susan C. Reinhard, Carol Levine, and Sarah Samis, "Employed Family Caregivers Providing Complex Chronic Care," AARP Public Policy Institute and United Hospital Fund, *Insight on the Issues* 86 (November 2013).

14. Francine Russo, *They're Your Parents Too!: How Siblings Can Survive Their Parents' Aging Without Driving Each Other Crazy* (New York: Bantam, 2010), 17.

15. Berit Ingersoll-Dayton et al., "Redressing Inequity in Parent Care Among Siblings," *Journal of Marriage and Family* 65, no. 1 (February 2003): 201–12; J. Jill Suitor and K. Pillemer, "Mothers' Favoritism in Later Life: The Role of Children's Birth Order," *Research on Aging* 29, no. 1 (January 2007): 32–55; and J. Jill Suitor et al., " 'I'm Sure She Chose Me!': Accuracy of Children's Reports of Mothers' Favoritism in Later Life Families," *Family Relations* 55, no. 5 (December 2006): 526–38.

16. National Alliance for Caregiving and AARP, *Caregiving in the United States 2009.*

17. EyerishLass, "Caregiving Broke My Spirit," Caregiver Action Network Forum, January 2013.

18. Jane Gross, "Dividing the Caregiving Duties, It's Daughters vs. Sons," "New Old Age" blog, *New York Times*, September 23, 2008, newoldage.blogs.nytimes.com/2008/09/23/in-the-nursing-home-its-daughters-v-sons.

19. National Alliance for Caregiving and AARP, *Caregiving in the United States 2009.*

20. Ann Bookman and Delia Kimbrel, "Families and Elder Care in the Twenty-First Century," *Future of Children* 21, no. 2 (Fall 2011): 128.

21. Hewitt Associates, *Work/Life Benefits Provided by Major U.S. Employers in 2003–2004* (Lincolnshire, IL: Hewitt Associates, 2003).

22. Society for Human Resource Management, *2007 Employee Benefits Survey* (Alexandria, VA: Society for Human Resource Management, 2007).

23. National Alliance for Caregiving and AARP, *Caregiving in the United States 2009*.

24. Center for Health Research, Healthways, Inc., and Joseph Coughlin, "Estimating the Impact of Caregiving and Employment on Well-Being," *Outcomes and Insights in Health Management*, May 2010, www.healthways.com /WorkArea/DownloadAsset.aspx?id=611.

25. Lynn Reinberg and Rita Choula, "Fact Sheet: Understanding the Impact of Family Caregiving on Work," AARP Public Policy Institute, October 2012, www.aarp.org/content/dam/aarp/research/public_policy_institute /ltc/2012/understanding-impact-family-caregiving-work-AARP-ppi-ltc.pdf.

3. The Caring Professionals

1. National Conference of State Legislatures and AARP Public Policy Institute, *Aging in Place* (Denver, CO: National Conference of State Legislatures; Washington, DC: AARP Public Policy Institute, 2011), http://assets .aarp.org/rgcenter/ppi/liv-com/aging-in-place-2011-full.pdf.

2. Quoted in Jane Gross, *A Bittersweet Season: Caring for Our Aging Parents—and Ourselves* (New York: Knopf, 2011), 164.

3. Laura Dresser and Adrienne Pagac, "Better Jobs for In-Home Direct Care Workers," Direct Care Alliance Policy Brief No. 5, October 2010, www .cows.org/_data/documents/1105.pdf.

4. Linda Burnham and Nik Theodore, *Home Economics: The Invisible and Unregulated World of Domestic Work* (New York: National Domestic Workers Alliance, 2012).

5. Institute for the Future of Aging Services, *The Long Term Care Workforce: Can the Crisis Be Fixed?* report prepared for the National Commission

for Quality Long-Term Care, January 2007, www.leadingage.org/uploaded Files/Content/About/Center_for_Applied_Research/Center_for_Applied _Research_Initiatives/LTC_Workforce_Commission_Report.pdf.

6. Burnham and Theodore, *Home Economics.*

7. Dowell Myers, Stephen Levy, and John Pitkin, *The Contributions of Immigrants and Their Children to the American Workforce and Jobs of the Future,* report for the Center for American Progress, June 19, 2013.

8. Dowell Myers, "Thinking Ahead About Our Immigrant Future: New Trends and Mutual Benefits in Our Aging Society," Immigration Policy Center, January 2008, www.immigrationpolicy.org/special-reports/thinking -ahead-about-our-immigrant-future-new-trends-and-mutual-benefits-our -aging-s.

9. According to the Board of Immigration Appeals: "When an alien-parent's child is a United States citizen and the child is below the age of discretion, and if the alien-parent is deported, it is the parent's decision whether to take the minor child along or to leave the child in this country." The U.S. Supreme Court affirmed that the Immigration and Naturalization Act "establishes that congressional concern was directed at 'the problem of keeping families of United States citizens and immigrants united.'" Both cited in *Shattered Families,* a report of the Applied Research Center, November 2011.

10. Gloria Steinem, *Moving Beyond Words* (New York: Simon & Schuster, 1994), 214–15.

11. Rohan Mascarenhas, "Care Work in America: An Interview with Nancy Folbre," Russell Sage Foundation, September 17, 2012, www.russellsage .org/blog/care-work-america-interview-nancy-folbre.

12. Arlie Hochschild, "Love and Gold," in "Valuing Domestic Work," ed. Gisela Fosada and Janet R. Jakobsen, special issue, *Scholar and Feminist Online* 8, no. 1 (Fall 2009), sfonline.barnard.edu/work/hochschild_01.htm.

13. "Fast Facts," National Center for Education Statistics, 2011, nces.ed .gov/fastfacts/display.asp?id=27.

14. Heather Boushey and Ann O'Leary, eds., *The Shriver Report 2009,* study by Maria Shriver and the Center for American Progress, October 2009, www .americanprogress.org/issues/2009/10/pdf/awn/a_womans_nation.pdf.

15. "Women CEOs of the Fortune 1000," Catalyst, May 1, 2014, www.catalyst.org/knowledge/women-ceos-fortune-1000.

16. Leslie Bennetts, "Women: The Invisible Poor," *Daily Beast*, September 14, 2011, www.thedailybeast.com/articles/2011/09/14/u-s-women-hit-hardest-by-poverty-says-census-report.html.

17. Mariko Chang, *Shortchanged: Why Women Have Less Wealth and What Can Be Done About It* (New York: Oxford University Press, 2010), 2.

Part II: Care at the Crossroads

1. Van Jones, conversation with the author, January 2013.

4. Waking the Caring Majority

1. Gary Orfield and Chungmei Lee, *Historic Reversals, Accelerating Resegregation, and the Need for New Integration Strategies*, Civil Rights Project, August 2007, civilrightsproject.ucla.edu/research/k-12-education/integration-and-diversity/historic-reversals-accelerating-resegregation-and-the-need-for-new-integration-strategies-1/orfield-historic-reversals-accelerating.pdf.

2. Richard Fry and Paul Taylor, "The Rise of Residential Segregation by Income," Pew Research and Social Trends, August 1, 2012, www.pewsocialtrends.org/2012/08/01/the-rise-of-residential-segregation-by-income/.

3. Nicole S. Dahmen and Raluca Cozma, eds., *Media Takes: On Aging* (New York: International Longevity Center; Sacramento: Aging Services of California, 2009).

4. Pema Chödrön, *When Things Fall Apart: Heart Advice for Difficult Times* (Boston: Shambhala Publications, 1997), 53.

5. "About the Elders," The Elders, theelders.org/about.

6. "About Us," Encore.org, www.encore.org/about.

7. "Inez Killingsworth," Encore.org, www.encore.org/inez-killingsworth.

8. "The Return of the Multi-Generational Family Household," Pew Research and Social Trends, March 18, 2010, www.pewsocialtrends.org/2010/03/18/the-return-of-the-multi-generational-family-household/.

9. "Millennials: Confident. Connected. Open to Change," Pew Research Center, February 24, 2010, www.pewsocialtrends.org/2010/02/24/millennials-confident-connected-open-to-change/.

10. Nikki Brown-Booker, testimony at a congressional briefing organized by Hand in Hand: The Domestic Employers Association, May 14, 2013.

11. Marjorie Dove Kent, "Honoring King, Fighting Fear: Why Economic Justice Must Matter to All Who Care About Racial Justice," Zeek, January 19, 2014, zeek.forward.com/articles/118011/.

12. Gail Sheehy, *Passages in Caregiving* (New York: William Morrow, 2010), 362.

13. Victor Quintana, interview with the author, March 28, 2014.

14. Emily A. Greenfield, Andrew E. Scharlach, Carrie L. Graham, Joan K. Davitt, and Amanda J. Lehning, "A National Overview of Villages: Results from a 2012 Organizational Survey," Rutgers School of Social Work, December 1, 2012.

15. Maurine Phinisee, interview with Paula Causey, Capitol Hill History Project, April 23, 2012, www.capitolhillhistory.org/interviews/2012/phinisee_maurine.html.

16. Sheehy, *Passages in Caregiving*, 363.

17. Ravi Dykema, "An Interview with Bernard Lietaer," *Nexus*, July–August 2003, www.nexuspub.com/articles_2003/interview_2003_ja.php.

18. The Caring Collaborative, Transition Network, www.thetransitionnetwork.org/connect/connect-caring-collaborative/.

5. A Policy of Caring

1. Joan Gage, "New Technology Helps with Eldercare—It's Not Just Robots," *Rolling Crone* blog, November 7, 2013, arollingcrone.blogspot.de/2013/11/new-technology-helps-with-eldercareits.html.

2. Mary Joe Gibson, "Lessons on Long-Term Care from Germany and Japan," in *Universal Coverage of Long-Term Care in the United States*, ed. Douglas A. Wolf and Nancy Folbre (New York: Russell Sage Foundation, 2012), 135.

3. "AARP Urges Budget Conference to Reject Harmful Cuts to Social Security and Medicare," letter from AARP to Chairman Patty Murray and Chairman Paul Ryan, November 1, 2013, www.aarp.org/about-aarp/press -center/info-11-2013/AARP-Urges-Budget-Conference-to-Reject-Harmful -Cuts.html.

4. Social Security Administration, *The 2013 Annual Report of the Board of Trustees of the Federal Old-Age and Survivors Insurance and Federal Disability Insurance Trust Funds*, May 31, 2013, 4, www.ssa.gov/oact/tr/2013/tr2013.pdf.

5. Virginia Reno and Joni Lavery, *Fixing Social Security* (Washington, DC: National Academy of Social Insurance, 2009), www.nasi.org/sites/default /files/research/Fixing_Social_Security.pdf.

6. Martin Luther King Jr. speaking at the Second National Convention of the Medical Committee for Human Rights, Chicago, March 25, 1966.

7. "PACE in the States," National PACE Association, www.npaonline .org/website/navdispatch.asp?id=1741.

8. Jane Gross, "Health Care Delivered as It Should Be," "New Old Age" blog, *New York Times*, January 8, 2009, newoldage.blogs.nytimes.com /2009/01/08/health-care-delivered-as-it-should-be.

9. "What Is PACE?" National PACE Association, www.npaonline.org /website/article.asp?id=12&title=Who,_What_and_Where_is_PACE?.

10. Geneva Association, *Health and Ageing* 13 (October 2005): 6–7.

11. Bipartisan Policy Center, "America's Long-Term Care Crisis: Challenges in Financing and Delivery," report, April 7, 2014, bipartisanpolicy.org /library/report/long-term-care-crisis.

12. Doris Meissner, Donald M. Kerwin, Muzaffar Chishti, and Claire Bergeron, *Immigration Enforcement in the United States* (Washington, DC: Migration Policy Institute, 2013).

13. Dean Baker, *The Savings from an Efficient Medicare Prescription Drug Plan* (Washington, DC: Center for Economic and Policy Research, 2006).

14. Rising Voices for a New Economy Summit, April 27, 2014, Washington, DC.

Appendix A: Government Programs Related to Aging and Care

1. AARP, "AARP to Congress and the President: Don't Cut Social Security," press release, December 18, 2012, www.aarp.org/about-aarp/press-center/info-12-2012/AARP-to-Congress-and-the-President-Dont-Cut-Social-Security.html.

2. Fifty-one percent of health care services, according to the Employee Benefit Research Institute. Cited in Paul Sullivan, "Planning for Retirement? Don't Forget Healthcare Costs," *New York Times*, October 5, 2012.

3. After a deductible, 100 percent of hospitalization costs are covered for the first sixty days; costs are shared after that.

4. Centers for Medicare & Medicaid Services, "Medicare Coverage of Skilled Nursing Facility Care," U.S. Department of Health and Human Services, January 2014, 5, www.medicare.gov/Pubs/pdf/10153.pdf.

5. After day 20 (days 21–100) with a co-pay from the patient.

Appendix B: Resources for Families

1. Department of Health and Human Services, Administration on Aging, Eldercare Locator, "Home Modifications," www.eldercare.gov/Eldercare .NET/Public/Resources/Factsheets/Home_Modifications.aspx.

2. Jane Gross, *A Bittersweet Season: Caring for Our Aging Parents—and Ourselves* (New York: Knopf, 2011), 120.

3. "Five Wishes," Aging with Dignity website, www.agingwithdignity .org/five-wishes.php.

INDEX

217

ABOUT THE AUTHORS

AI-JEN POO is the director of the National Domestic Workers Alliance (NDWA) and a co-director of Caring Across Generations. She began organizing immigrant women workers in 1996 and has helped launch several initiatives that have secured basic protections for domestic workers, such as New York State's Domestic Workers' Bill of Rights.

In 2007, together with fifty women from around the country, Poo helped found NDWA, the leading organization working to bring respect and dignity to our nation's growing workforce of nannies, housekeepers, and caregivers for the aging, and has served as the director since 2010. In 2011, she co-founded Caring Across Generations, a movement inspiring people to value connections across generations and promoting policies protecting the dignity and independence of seniors, people with disabilities, and workers who care for them.

A graduate of Columbia College, Poo is a World Economic Forum Young Global Leader and currently serves on the boards of several organizations, including Momsrising.org and the National Council on Aging. She is the recipient of numerous awards, including the Woman of Vision Award from the Ms. Foundation for Women and the Independent Sector American Express NGen

Leadership Award, and was named one of *Time*'s "100 Most Influential People in the World" in 2012 and a MacArthur Fellow in 2014. Her work has been featured in *Marie Claire*, the *New York Times*, the *Washington Post*, *Time*, *Jezebel*, CNN.com, and elsewhere. She is a practitioner of Ashtanga yoga and currently lives in Chicago.

ARIANE CONRAD is a narrative strategist known as the Book Doula. She worked with American environmental advocate and civil rights activist Van Jones on two *New York Times* bestsellers, *The Green Collar Economy* and *Rebuild the Dream*, and with the economic reformer and waste activist Annie Leonard on *The Story of Stuff*.

ABOUT THE PHOTOGRAPHERS

MICHELE ASSELIN, a photographer based in Los Angeles, is known for her formal portraiture, which examines individual identities within larger social constructs. After studying comparative literature and political science, she moved to Jerusalem to work for the Associated Press. There she covered current events, primarily in the Gaza Strip and the West Bank. After her stay in Jerusalem, Asselin moved to back to the States to focus on photographic portraiture. While living in New York, she began her career as an editorial photographer. Her work has been featured in the *New Yorker*, the *New York Times Magazine*, *Time*, *Esquire*, and *Wired*, among other publications. Some of her recent series, shot for exhibition, have focused on domestic labor, personal identity, and disappearing communities.

ALESSANDRA SANGUINETTI was born in New York in 1968 and lived in Argentina from 1970 until 2003. Currently based in San Francisco, she is a recipient of generous fellowships and prizes, including a Guggenheim fellowship, a Hasselblad Foundation grant, and a Robert Gardner Fellowship in Photography. She is a member of Magnum Photos and is represented in New York by Yossi Milo Gallery and in Buenos Aires by Galeria Ruth Benzacar.

Publishing in the Public Interest

Thank you for reading this book published by The New Press. The New Press is a nonprofit, public interest publisher. New Press books and authors play a crucial role in sparking conversations about the key political and social issues of our day.

We hope you enjoyed this book and that you will stay in touch with The New Press. Here are a few ways to stay up to date with our books, events, and the issues we cover:

- Sign up at www.thenewpress.com/subscribe to receive updates on New Press authors and issues and to be notified about local events
- Like us on Facebook: www.facebook.com/newpressbooks
- Follow us on Twitter: www.twitter.com/thenewpress

Please consider buying New Press books for yourself; for friends and family; or to donate to schools, libraries, community centers, prison libraries, and other organizations involved with the issues our authors write about.

The New Press is a 501(c)(3) nonprofit organization. You can also support our work with a tax-deductible gift by visiting www.thenewpress.com/donate.